ENDLESS PATH

# Aztec

This is a **FLAME TREE** book
First published in 2006

Publisher and Creative Director: Nick Wells
Designer: Jake
Project Editor: Catherine Emslie
Picture Researcher: Gemma Walters
Production: Kelly Fenlon, Chris Herbert and Claire Walker

**FLAME TREE PUBLISHING**
Crabtree Hall, Crabtree Lane
Fulham, London SW6 6TY
United Kingdom
www.flametreepublishing.com

06 08 10 09 07
1 3 5 7 9 10 8 6 4 2

Flame Tree is part of The Foundry Creative Media Company Limited
Copyright © The Foundry 2006

A copy of the CIP data for this book is available from the British Library.

ISBN-10: 1-84451-515-X
ISBN-13: 978-1-84451-515-8

Every effort has been made to contact copyright holders. In the event of an oversight
the publishers would be glad to rectify any omissions in future editions of this book.

Printed in China

ENDLESS PATH

# Aztec

Author: Rachel Storm          Foreword: Dr Nicholas J. Saunders

**FLAME TREE**
**PUBLISHING**

# Contents

## The Land of the Feathered Serpent: Religion and Belief ..218

# Foreword: Mesoamerica

Mesoamerica is a cultural area, not a geographical place. It is a name given by archaeologists and anthropologists to describe a region of Central America that includes modern Mexico, Guatemala, Belize, Honduras, and parts of El Salvador, Nicaragua and Costa Rica. The ancient peoples who lived in this geographically diverse region – from deserts to mountains and tropical rainforests – shared common traits of civilisation for some three thousand years, between 1500 BC and the Spanish conquest of AD 1519–21. Despite their differences in language, politics, art styles, and ethnic identity, these societies held in common such features as hieroglyphic writing, a hierarchical pantheon of gods, a 260-day sacred calendar, a rubber-ball game, pyramid-temple building, and an agricultural system based on corn (maize), beans, and squash. Many of their myths were also similar, especially in the ways that they legitimized the organization of society, and stressed the role of their royal rulers as leaders chosen and supported by the gods. Mesoamerica's vibrant mix of similarity and difference gave rise to one of the most stunning and sophisticated civilizations of the ancient world.

The origins of Mesoamerican culture began around 2000 BC, but it was Mexico's precocious Olmec society, beginning around 1250 BC, that first crystallized all the different features into a recognizable civilization. Building on the agricultural and settled village life that preceded them, the Olmecs forged Mesoamerica's first major art style, created a religion with identifiable gods, and constructed the first ceremonial architecture in the form of an earthen pyramid and several large settlements dominated by monumental sculptures. Binding this together was a sophisticated ideology that used images of a fierce jaguar creature that was associated with the rulers of Olmec society. These developments set a new course for human societies in prehistoric Mexico, and that soon became a pan-Mesoamerican phenomenon.

The Olmecs played a unique and pivotal role in the rise of Mesoamerican civilization, and are often called the 'Mother Culture' of ancient Mesoamerica. In fact, the development of civilization was a complex process, with different features occurring at different times across a large area. Between 1500 BC and 1000 BC, on the Pacific coast, and in the central Mexican highlands, early sites such as La Victoria and Tlatilco have yielded technically brilliant pottery and 'crying' baby-face figurines. At San José Mogote, in the Valley of Oaxaca (home to the later Zapotecs), there was an intense production of shiny mirrors, perhaps used in religious rituals, that were exchanged with the great Olmec centres further east. Trade was probably one mechanism by which the influence of Mesoamerican civilization spread across such a vast area.

The Olmecs, it seems, were crucially important in defining Mesoamerican civilization, but did not invent it alone. They produced art inspired by an ancient and magical worldview, where humans and animals shared souls and appearances, and where the landscapes of snow-capped volcanoes and lush jungles were infused with the spirits of ancestors. In pottery, jade, sculpture and painting, Olmec craftsmen gave an enduring physical shape to ancient ideas and beliefs. Mesoamerican civilization, however, was a hybrid creation, where different peoples borrowed, exchanged, and adapted ideas and objects to create something distinctive and new.

Such was the influence of the Olmec people, that the great Mesoamerican civilizations of the Zapotecs, Maya, Teotihuacans, Huastecs, Toltecs, and Aztecs, all shared its underlying view of a spiritually connected and animated world. At their mountain-top city of Monte Alban, the Zapotecs developed a hieroglyphic writing system to record historical events and measure the passing of time in a curious double calendar (one sacred, the other secular) that would be borrowed and adapted by many later Mesoamerican civilizations. Human sacrifice and the sacred power of human blood offered to the gods featured widely in Zapotec culture, and became a vital part of Maya religious rituals, where new kings sanctified their positions through bloody rites of accession and warfare. Great Maya cities such as Tikal, Palenque, and Copan abound with hieroglyphic inscriptions and sculptures announcing the blood-soaked legitimacy of their kings. Aztec religion, too, stressed the importance of offering one's own blood (as well as that of others) to the gods, to provide them with nourishment and the strength to keep the world in motion.

These features of Mesoamerican civilization were bound together by sacred myths, where gods and heroes fought and died to create and recreate the world in different versions. Time and space were bound together through beliefs in the religious significance of the appearance and movements of the sun, moon, and stars – and which were reflected in the layout of cities like Teotihuacan, and the Aztec capital of Tenochtitlan. The Mesoamerican world was a dazzling expression of indigenous American civilization that had developed in isolation from the rest of the planet for millennia. It is no surprise that it was a strange and alien place to the Spanish who encountered and conquered it barely five hundred years ago.

Dr Nicholas J. Saunders, 2006
Reader in Material Culture, University College London

# Mesoamerica: A Melting Pot of Cultures

# Mesoamerica

Thousands of years ago one of the world's earliest civilisations arose in a region of central America known as Mesoamerica. Geographically, Mesoamerica covers most of present-day Mexico, Guatemala, Belize, El Salvador and western Honduras. It divides roughly into two parts: central Mexico west and north of the Isthmus of Tehuantepec, which connects the Atlantic and Pacific oceans, and the Maya region to the east and south including the Yucatán Peninsula. Culturally, Mesoamerican civilization is considered to last up until the Spanish conquest in the sixteenth century although its influence can still be felt today.

Mesoamerica

## Climate and Culture

The climate of Mesoamerica varies hugely, ranging from deserts in the north to tropical rainforests in the south. Many different peoples lived in the region, sometimes peacefully side by side, sometimes locked in war. Despite this, a surprisingly unified body of religious beliefs, thought, architecture, art and social organization diffused throughout the area.

# The Olmecs

By about 1500 BC the hunter-gatherer way of life had almost disappeared across Mesoamerica and village life, supported by farming, had become established. Sometime after 1200 BC, the Olmec civilization arose on the hot and humid eastern coast of Mexico, mainly around Tabasco and Veracruz. The Olmecs are sometimes known as the 'mother culture' of Mesoamerica because of their influence on later groups across the region. Through trading networks, Olmec influence spread out southwards to Guatemala and north to the Valley of Mexico. The Olmecs were a highly developed, well-organized people. They are thought to have developed a complex calendar and religious system as well as ceremonial centres. They may also have used a very early form of writing, and possibly developed the idea of a plumed serpent, a symbol which was to be of major importance throughout Mesoamerica. Sometime after 450 BC, Olmec influence began to wane but by now the culture of these people had set a lasting mark on the entire region.

## The Rubber People

Nobody knows what the Olmec people called themselves. The word 'Olmec' is Nahuatl for 'rubber people' and was given to the civilization centuries after its demise, possibly because the region was known for a type of rubber tree. The word might, on the other hand, refer to the rubber balls used in the famous Mesoamerican ball games which the Olmecs may have introduced.

# The Huastecs

The Huastec people settled in north-eastern Mexico, north of Veracruz, sometime around 1250 BC. Although they spoke a Mayan language, they were never part of Mayan culture. They were instantly recognizable for their custom of wearing conical hats, often their sole item of clothing — although they also wore elaborate costumes. Circular and conical buildings are also found in Huastec regions. The Huastecs helped to bring about the downfall of the Toltec empire (*see* page 47) but they themselves were defeated by the Aztecs in the mid-fifteenth century and forced to pay tribute. Eventually they were conquered by the Spanish in the sixteenth century.

# The Zapotecs

Zapotec culture arose in
south-western Mexico
around 500 BC and lasted
until nearly the end of the
fifteenth century when
the Zapotec people were
assimilated into the
Aztec Empire.

## Cloud People

The Aztecs named the Zapotecs after
a legend which tells of their descent
from the zapote tree. The elite
Zapotecs, however, claimed to be
descended from supernatural beings
who lived high among the clouds and
called themselves the 'cloud people'.

## Princess Coyolicatzin

According to legend, after several years of war between the Aztecs and Zapotecs, the Aztec emperor Ahuizotl made a proposal to the Zapotec king Cosihuesa of Tehuantepec. Ahuizotl, who admired his enemy, wanted to form an alliance, and so offered Cosihuesa an Aztec princess, Coyolicatzin, as his bride. Unsure what to do, Cosihuesa hurried off to bathe at a spa in order that he might mull over the proposal. It was there that Princess Coyolicatzin eventually found the king and her charms so impressed him that they married and the Zapotecs and Aztecs finally formed an alliance. Time passed and eventually the old animosity between the two peoples arose once more. One night, the Aztecs attacked Cosihuesa's city expecting Coyolicatzin to open the gates for them. To their surprise, the queen refused, siding instead with her husband and the Zapotec people.

# The Totonacs

Along the eastern coast of Mexico, occupying a
region which more or less corresponds with the
modern state of Veracruz, a highly advanced
culture arose which is called either Totonac or
Classic Veracruz. The Aztecs called the Totonac
region Totonacapa. Towards the end of the
fifteenth century, the Totonacs were conquered by
the Aztecs and forced to pay a huge tribute of
cloth, maize, honey and wax to the Aztec capital
Tenochtitlan. When the Spanish conqueror
Hernán Cortés landed near Veracruz, the Totonacs
saw their chance to rid themselves of this burden
and joined forces with the Spanish, eventually
overcoming the Aztecs.

# Teotihuacan

The settlement of Teotihuacan began to take shape in the second century BC in the Valley of Mexico. Situated close to a series of springs and to obsidian mines, it was ideally placed for irrigation-based farming, trade and the manufacture of tools and knives. From the beginning of the first century AD, a huge building effort began and Teotihuacan came to dominate Mesoamerica, remaining important until around AD 600. At its peak the city had a population of more than one hundred thousand. Nobody knows where the Teotihuacans came from, nor what the city was originally called. The Aztecs regarded it as their ancestral home and called it Teotihuacan 'Birthplace of the Gods' long after its collapse.

## The Collapse of the City

Teotihuacan's demise came suddenly. Around AD 650 violence broke out in certain areas of the city, quite why or at whose hands nobody knows, though internal dissension or revolt had probably arisen. Teotihuacan's reign was over, although the city continued to be regarded as a spiritual centre. When the site was examined centuries later, dismembered skeletons were found lying in the rooms close to the Ciudadela, the large enclosure at the centre of the city. The skulls of these skeletons were broken and their bodies had been cut into pieces. Some of the skeletons still wore beautiful jewellery and ornaments of jade and shell. The floors of the rooms where they lay were littered with broken pieces of pottery, sculptures, braziers and roof decorations. However, the rooms where the poor people lived remained untouched. Perhaps this indicates that the common people had rebelled against their superiors. Or perhaps there is some other answer.

# The Mixtecs

The Mixtecs called themselves 'the people of the rain', reflecting the climate of their early hilltop settlements in what is now north-western Oaxaca. Sometime around the ninth century they moved south, spreading throughout Oaxaca, Puebla and Guerrero. It is from this time until the early sixteenth century that Mixtec culture truly flourished. The Mixtecs were fierce warriors as well as skilled craftspeople. Their region was divided into numerous territories each with its own leading family and these clans fought against each other as well as joining together to fight their Zapotec rivals. They eventually won the important cities of Mitla and Monte Alban from the Zapotecs and set their distinctive stylistic stamp on both places. In order to overcome the Aztecs they briefly joined forces with the Zapotecs but the Zapotecs eventually sided with the Aztecs and then with the Spanish. The Mixtecs continued to resist the Spanish until they were finally conquered by Pedro de Alvarado.

# The Tarascans

The Tarascan or Purepecha people flourished in western Mexico around Lake Patzcuaro in Michoacan. They eventually established an empire which at its height, sometime around AD 1400, was second in size only to the Aztec empire. It was regarded by the Spanish conquerors as the most advanced culture in the entire region. The Tarascans had well-organized border guards and fortifications. They were the only Mesoamericans to succeed in preventing the Aztecs from taking over their territory even though they made several attempts to do so. As a result the Tarascans retained their own unique artistic culture, drawing for resources on a region rich in copper, gold, silver, obsidian and onyx. At its peak, the Tarascan capital, Tzintzuntzan, had a population of about 35,000. In 1522 the last Tarascan king, Tangaxoan II surrendered to the Spanish.

## The Legend of Princess Erendira

Princess Erendira, the 16-year-old daughter of the Tarascan king Tangaxoan II, was devastated when she heard that her father had surrendered to the Spanish. Undaunted, however, she set up camp on a hilltop and prepared to lead the Tarascans into battle against the Conquistadors. Single-handedly, the princess killed a Spanish soldier, seized his horse and used it to train her followers to ride. While she was away fighting, a small band of Spanish soldiers crept up to Erendira's hilltop camp and killed the king, who was lying there sick and frail. As soon as Erendira heard what had happened, she rushed to her father. At this point, tales of what happened to the princess next vary. Some say that she left the region in order to train other warriors; others say that she killed herself after falling in love with a Spanish monk.

# The Maya

The Maya lived in the eastern third of Mesoamerica, in southern Mexico, Guatemala and northern Belize, but mainly on the Yucatán Peninsula. Mayan civilization is usually divided into three time periods stretching over 3,000 years. The Pre-Classic (2000 BC to AD 250) was the period in which the Maya settled in villages and began farming (mainly maize, beans and squash) and building. The Classic Period ran from AD 250 to AD 900 and was the time in which the Maya's stunning ceremonial centres flourished with their ball courts, temples, pyramids and palaces. Eventually, the Maya controlled more than 40 cities each, with a population of between 5,000 and 50,000. The Post-Classic Period lasted from AD 900 to AD 1500. Its beginning is marked by a sudden decline in Mayan civilization. Many cities were abandoned and became overgrown. Some, however, such as Chichen Itza and Mayapan, continued to thrive.

## The Fall of the Cities

Many reasons have been given for the sudden abandonment of Mayan cities and the collapse of Mayan urban society. It is possible that the soil became exhausted, that water supplies dried up, that an earthquake occurred or that disease broke out. Still, no one knows for sure. One of the most persuasive arguments is that the Maya became victims of their own success. In the larger cities, which were the first to collapse, it is possible that the elites became so powerful and so numerous and demanded so much tribute that the commoners eventually fled, causing the once highly organized society to disintegrate.

# The Toltecs

After the fall of Teotihuacan in the seventh century AD, a long period of instability occurred throughout much of Mesoamerica. Sometime around AD 900, a trading base situated north of what is now Mexico City developed into a centralizing force in the region. This centre, called Tula or Place of the Reeds, eventually came to be the capital of the huge Toltec empire which reached across Mexico, Guatemala and the Yucatán Peninsula. The Toltecs, a word meaning something like 'urbanite' or 'reed people', were fearsomely warlike and used their military strength to dominate anyone who stood in their way. However, when civil war broke out at the end of the tenth century, the Toltec empire collapsed. Although legend and history often become intertwined in the story of the Toltecs, it seems that one faction broke away and marched off to the east, eventually establishing itself at the Mayan city of Chichen Itza.

# The Pipils

When the Spanish arrived in El Salvador in the sixteenth century, the first and most powerful people they encountered there were the Pipils. Although other people at other times have been known by the same name, these El Salvadorean Pipils may be descended from the powerful Toltecs. One theory holds that they arrived in El Salvador around the year AD 1000 following the collapse of the Toltec empire. The Pipils called their home Cuzcatlan, 'Land of Richness'; they founded at least two city states and worshipped the rain god Tlaloc and Xipe Totec, the god of sacrifice. The Pipils also established a flourishing trade network dealing in woven goods and agricultural products including cocoa and indigo.

# The Aztecs

In about AD 1100 a group of Nahuatl-speaking people began to migrate

southwards towards central Mexico. They were called the Mexica after Mexi, a

legendary ancient priest. Around AD 1325, the Mexica finally settled on a marshy

island in the basin of Lake Texcoco. There, they built a sanctuary dedicated to their

god Huitzilopochtli and to Tlaloc, god of rain. Nearly 50 years later a powerful

neighbouring city called Azcapotzalco took control of Tenochtitlan. In AD 1427,

Tenochtitlan teamed up with two smaller city-states, Tlacopan which was situated

on the west shore of Lake Texcoco and Texcoco which lay to the east of the

lake. Together, the three cities formed the Triple Alliance and defeated

Azcapotzalco. The Mexica of Tenochtitlan soon became the dominant force

of the Triple Alliance and the Aztec empire began.

## The Place of Whiteness

The word Aztec means 'People from Aztlan', the
mythical homeland of the Mexica people. In Nahuatl,
the language spoken by the Mexica and other
Mesoamerican peoples, Aztlan means 'Place of the
Heron' or 'Place of Whiteness'.

## The Empire

In the 90 years it reigned before being defeated by the Spanish, the Triple Alliance forged an empire with a population of somewhere between five and six million people that stretched from the Gulf Coast to the Pacific and from Central Mexico to the Isthmus of Tehuantepec. This empire was taken by force: the Aztecs tended to kill, take prisoners and impose large tribute payments on conquered people. They would also sacrifice them in awe-inspiring rituals, which, despite being in a mytho-cosmological-religious context, were mainly to inspire terror and respect in the hearts of their enemies.

## The Legend

According to Aztec lore, their ancestors emerged from the bowels of the earth through seven caves known as Chicomoztoc. They settled somewhere in the distant north, on an island called Aztlan, the Place of Whiteness. One day, sometime towards the end of the twelfth century, the Aztec sun god Huitzilopochtli, Blue Humming Bird of the South, the god of war and power, spoke to his people from the ruins of a temple. He sent them on a pilgrimage which was to last nearly a century, promising them that one day they would find a cactus growing on a rock on an island in a lake. Standing on top of the cactus they would see their god in the form of a shining golden eagle holding a serpent in its talons. This would be the place where they were to settle and where they were to build a city from which they would rule all Mexico.

## The Journey

The Aztecs set off on their journey southwards in eight groups. Accompanying them were four tribal leaders or god-bearers, one of whom carried an image of Huitzilopochtli. Now and again, Huitzilopochtli would speak to his people, giving them advice. After suffering great hardships, the Aztecs were defeated in battle and taken captive by the king of Colhuacan. The king soon sent the tough Aztec warriors to fight in a battle against a neighbouring tribe. He allowed them no weapons, only their bare hands and what sticks and stones they could find. The Aztecs killed every single enemy warrior they saw, cutting an ear from each victim and gathering all the ears into great bags. When the king called the Aztecs to him, the mighty warriors emptied out a heap of human ears at his feet. The king was shocked and afraid. He dismissed the Aztecs, allowing them freedom to settle wherever they desired.

### The Place of the Cactus Fruit

The Aztecs set off along the shore of Lake Texcoco until they came to a rocky island hidden in the swamps. There, the Aztec leader found a stream beside a rock and on the rock stood a cactus bearing red fruit. A shining eagle, symbol of the sun, perched on top of the cactus. At this very moment, Huitzilopochtli called out: 'O Mexica, it shall be here!' The Aztecs' long pilgrimage was over. The year was 1325. It was there that the Aztecs founded the city of Tenochtitlan, the heart of the Aztec empire, the 'place of the cactus fruit'.

# Pyramids, Temples and Cities:
## Architecture and Infrastructure

# Pyramids

Mesoamerican pyramids are usually stepped and have a platform or temple at their summit. They were generally built of earth and faced with stone. A large pyramid might have taken around 30 years to build and would have required a workforce of thousands. Whereas some Mesoamerican pyramids were, like Egyptian pyramids, elaborate tombs, the main function of Mesoamerican pyramids was to act as vast stages for public ceremonies, particularly religious rituals. Egyptian pyramids were situated away from towns and villages but Mesoamerican pyramids were located at city centres. They were part of people's everyday experience and played an important role in society, reminding people constantly of their relationship to the gods. They were a reminder, too, of the price that would have to be paid should they break the rules of their society, since most sacrifices took place either on the square facing the pyramid or on the pyramid platform.

# Talud Tablero

The most well-known Mesoamerican architectural style is called *talud-tablero*. It was used by many different cultures in the region, notably in Monte Alban and Teotihuacan. The style consists of a sloping wall called the *talud* with the *tablero*, a flat slab, placed on top. In Teotihuacan, the Temple of Quetzalcoatl is designed in a six-tiered *talud-tablero* style.

# San Lorenzo

San Lorenzo is the Olmecs' earliest known ceremonial centre. It dates from about 1450 BC and at its height was populated by about 15,000 people. As well as being an important religious site, farmers and artisans lived there. Situated along Mexico's fertile Gulf Coast, San Lorenzo was ideally placed for trade and communications. It was originally built on a low hill which was later enlarged to form a vast platform on which smaller earthen platforms were built to support temples and palaces, mostly made of wood. The houses of commoners, made from wood, clay and palm leaves, were built on terraces set into the sides of the large mound. San Lorenzo also had a drainage system consisting of underground drains made from basalt. The stone would have been brought down from the Tuxtla mountains about 60 miles away to the north, probably by means of rivers.

# La Venta

La Venta lay east of San Lorenzo on a small island in the coastal swamp. It became the Olmecs' most important city in about 900 BC and remained so until it was abandoned in about 400 BC. Like San Lorenzo, La Venta was built on and around a raised mound where religious rituals were held. The Great Pyramid at La Venta stood some 30 m (98 ft) high and is one of Mesoamerica's earliest pyramids. It may have originally had stepped sides, a hallmark of Mesoamerican architecture, allowing the priests to climb upwards 'towards the gods', but over time these earthen steps will have probably. The pyramid divided La Venta into north and south. To the north lay the ceremonial centre, which was probably reserved for the Olmec elite, while to the south lay a vast plaza which may have been where the rulers performed their elaborate rituals. Many splendid treasures have been uncovered at La Venta including buried offerings of serpentine and jade.

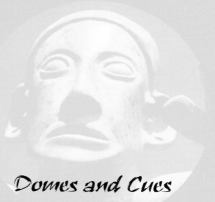

# Domes and Cues

The Huastecs built round, domed or circular monuments. In the north of Veracruz, they were also known for building earth mounds called *cues*.

# Mitla

The Zapotec city of Mitla ('Place of the Dead') was probably originally intended as a sacred burial site. In about AD 1000 it was conquered by the Mixtecs who created the astounding Group of Columns, the largest of five clusters of buildings, three of which (including the Group of Columns) were probably palaces and two of which were ceremonial centres. More than 500 years later, after the Spanish Conquest, a colonial church was built inside one of the palace structures. Today, during fiestas, Zapotec ceremonies are still held there alongside Christian rituals. According to legend, anyone who embraces the Column of Life in Mitla's Hall of Columns will discover from the space left between their hands how long they have left to live.

# Monte Alban

The Zapotec capital city and ceremonial centre, Monte Alban, dates back to about 500 BC or earlier. It is dramatically situated on top of a hill in the Valley of Oaxaca in southern Mexico. In order to build it, the entire top of the hill was levelled. Afterwards, a vast plaza was created, flanked by temples, pyramids and other buildings, including a ballcourt. The ordinary people lived on terraces cut into the hillside below the ceremonial centre. The Temple of Danzantes was probably the earliest monument in Monte Alban. It is faced with hundreds of great slabs carved with naked, distorted and sometimes mutilated male figures, probably intended to depict prisoners caught by the Zapotecs in battle. At its height, from around AD 500–900, Monte Alban had a population of more than 25,000. After about AD 900 the city was more or less abandoned. The Mixtecs used the tombs for their dead, though they did not occupy the city.

# El Tajin

The city of El Tajin on the Gulf Coast may have been the Totanacs' capital city. At its height, sometime after AD 750, it had a population of about 20,000. With a total of 17 ballcourts and hundreds of ballgame sculptures, the game clearly dominated the city, probably serving a ritual function. El Tajin was both a working city and a religious centre with a sophisticated, hierarchical society and, at its centre, many temple complexes. At its height, from AD 600–900, it boasted hundreds of houses surrounded by gardens and fruit trees. The Pyramid of the Niches looms over the lower ceremonial centre of the city. In all, it has 346 little openings, each roughly 60 cm (24 in) deep. These niches might have formed part of a giant calendar.

# Teotihuacan

Teotihuacan (City of the Gods) is organized along a central north-south axis known as the Street of the Dead which extends for about 5 km (3.1 miles). At its centre stands the Sun Pyramid, Teotihuacan's largest monument, while the Moon Pyramid stands at its northern end. The Street of the Dead is crossed at right angles by the East-West Avenue, also 5 km (3.1 miles) long. The city was thus divided into quadrants and was laid out on a grid pattern, filled with hundreds of apartment compounds. Some houses were built of stone and decorated with murals whereas the poorer farmers lived in wooden houses. A huge sunken enclosure known as the *ciudadela* or citadel was situated where the Street of the Dead crosses the East-West Avenue, with the Feathered Serpent Pyramid as its focal point — in all there were about 600 pyramids in the city. The city's elite lived close to the citadel.

## Teotihuacan Sun Pyramid

In 1971 archaeologists discovered that
Teotihuacan's Sun Pyramid had been built over a
natural, tunnel-like cave which led to chambers
where fire and water rituals were conducted. The
cave may have been seen as a gateway to the
spiritual world as well as the place from which the
first humans emerged.

# Yacatas

The Tarascans' most disctinctive buildings are known as *yacatas*. They are stepped pyramids, usually T-shaped, consisting of three parts: a rectangular stepped pyramid, a circular stepped pyramid and a stepped passageway. Five *yacatas* stood at the ceremonial centre of the Tarascan capital Tzintzuntzan. Some of the Tzintzuntzan *yacatas* are rectangular, some oval or circular and others are in the typical Tarascan T-shape. These buildings seem to have been used both as dwellings and as burial places. Apart from the *yacatas*, there was a notable lack of monumental building across the Tarascan empire.

# Tula

Tula, the Toltecs' ancient capital, is situated in the Mexican state of Hildago, near the modern town of Tula de Allende. It rose to power after the collapse of Teotihuacan and flourished from about AD 980 until it collapsed, possibly due to drought and famine, sometime around AD 1168–79. At its height, the city had a population of at least 30,000. Today, it is famous for its giant stone warriors known as the Atlantes.

# Stelae

Large standing stones known as *stelae* were common throughout the Mayan empire. The stones were carved with long hieroglyphic texts which commemorated important historical events such as battles and genealogies. The most famous *stelae* are situated in the ancient city of Copan in Honduras. The Maya called the *stelae* '*tetun*' or 'tree stones'.

# Tikal

Deep in the tropical rainforests of Guatemala, the Maya built Tikal, the
largest of their great ceremonial centres. There were settlements in the
region as far back as 800 BC, but it was not until 750 AD that Tikal reached its
peak. In all, the city boasted 3,000 buildings including six limestone pyramids, as
well as numerous palaces and ballcourts. Archaeologists have also unearthed
somewhere around 100,000 tools, ceremonial objects and personal ornaments at
the site. At the centre of the city lies the Great Plaza next to which stand
acropolises and temples. In front of the north acropolis (the city's religious centre)
about 70 *stelae* were lined up. Many were decorated with carvings and had
altars set in front of them. At its height, Tikal had a population of between 45,000
and 75,000. During the early Classic Period, the city played an important part in
the trading networks established by Teotihuacan. Like other lowland Mayan sites,
Tikal was abandoned around AD 900.

# Chichen Itza

Following the collapse of many Mayan cities in the ninth century, particularly in the south, the Maya of the north began to view Chichen Itza in Yucatan as their capital. The city's ruins can be divided into two main groups: those belonging to the Mayan period were built between the sixth and tenth centuries AD while those belonging to the Mayan Toltec period date from the late tenth century when a Mayan group heavily influenced and perhaps led by Toltecs, invaded the city. Chichen Itza finally collapsed after being attacked in the early thirteenth century; a new capital was founded at Mayapan.

## El Caracol

The monument at Chichen Itza known as *El Caracol* (The Snail) earns its name from its inner, winding staircase. It was probably used as an observatory. Stars and planets can be seen through particular windows on certain dates. For example, the three windows in the higher tower would have looked out to Venus rising at its southern and northern extremes and at the sunset on the equinox.

## El Castillo

One of the most famous monuments at Chichen Itza is the Temple of Kukulkan, known as El Castillo (The Castle). Built sometime before AD 800, it is a square-based, stepped pyramid standing 27.5 m (90 ft) high. The temple embodies information about the Mayan calendar. Each side of the pyramid has 52 rectangular panels, equal to the number of years in the Mayan calendar, and each of the pyramid's four staircases has 91 steps which, together with the platform's step at the very top, adds up to 365, the number of days in the solar year.

# Palenque and Uxmal

Other important Mayan centres included Palenque in the Mexican state of Chiapas and Uxmal in the state of Yucatan. They both feature a range of well-preserved, impressive structures from the Pyramid of the Magician at Uxmal, to the Temple of Inscriptions at Palenque.

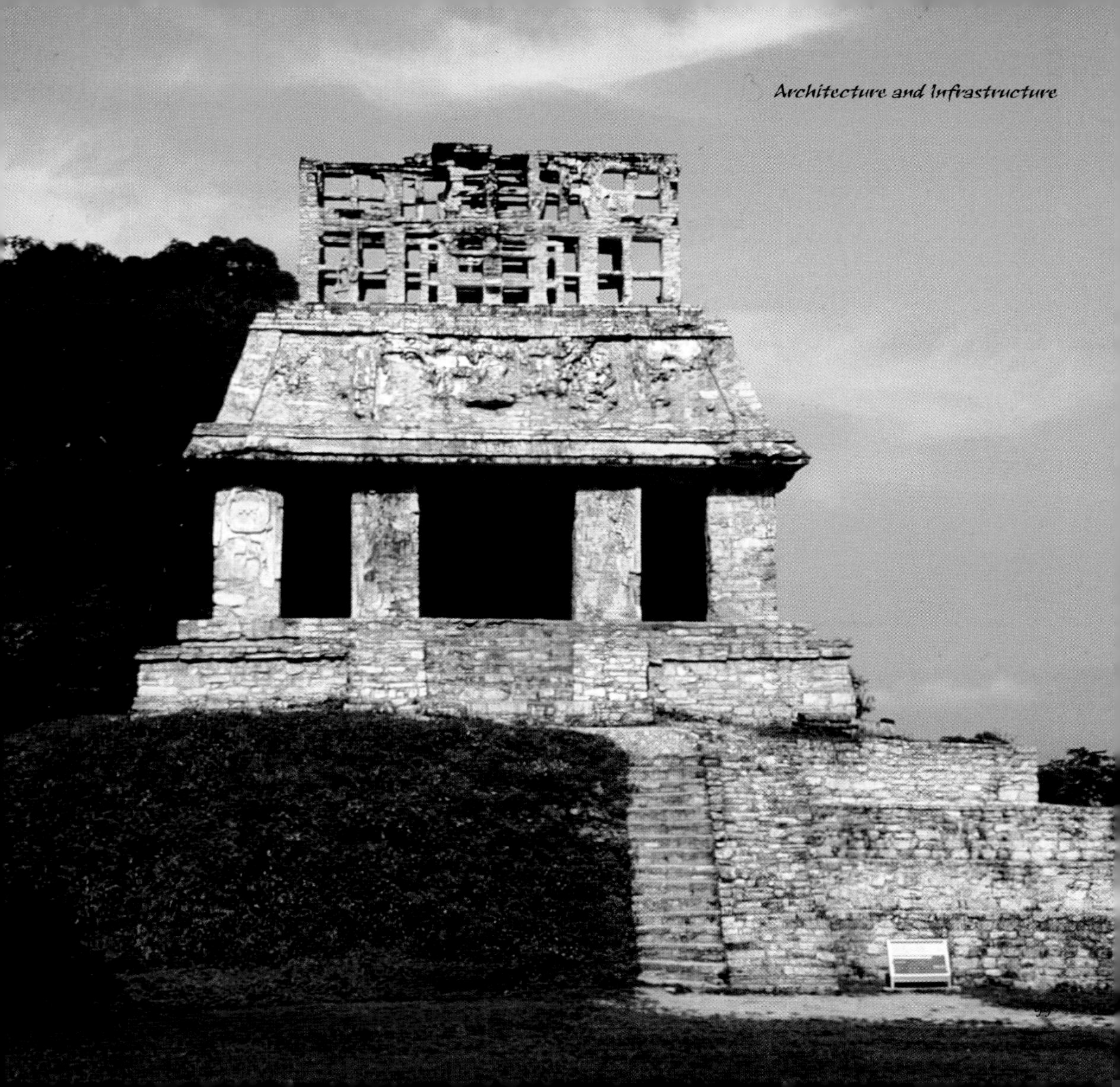

# Tenochtitlan

Tenochtitlan, the Aztec capital, grew from a small settlement in the swamps of the shallow Lake Texcoco to one of the largest cities in the world. The Aztecs regarded it as their *axis mundi*, the centre of their sacred universe. The Spanish conquerors called it the 'Venice of the New World'. The city was built on five islands that were connected to the mainland by three causeways. Streets and canals were laid out according to a grid pattern and two aqueducts supplied the city with fresh water. There were beautiful palaces painted white, awesome pyramids painted red and blue and busy marketplaces selling an exotic range of goods. In the Sacred Precinct, the ceremonial centre of Tenochtitlan, stood the temples of the most important Aztec gods, as well as a ballcourt and schools for training young nobles for the priesthood. The focus of the centre was the Templo Mayor or Great Pyramid.

## The Templo Mayor

The Templo Mayor was a double pyramid that stood at the very centre of Tenochtitlan. As soon as the Aztecs arrived at the site of their future city, they built a basic shrine to their tribal god, Huitzilopochtli. From these humble beginnings the magnificent Templo Mayor arose. At about 30 m (98 ft) high, it stood taller than all the other buildings in the city and consisted of two stepped pyramids, each symbolizing a sacred mountain. One pyramid was intended to represent the Hill of Coatepec where Huitzilopochtli was said to have been born; the other symbolized the Hill of Sustenance whose patron deity was the rain god Tlaloc. Temples at the top of each of the pyramids housed images of these two gods and were reached by wide, balustraded staircases. The Templo Mayor was re-built about seven times, usually because the ground on which it stood was unstable. It was also enlarged 11 times.

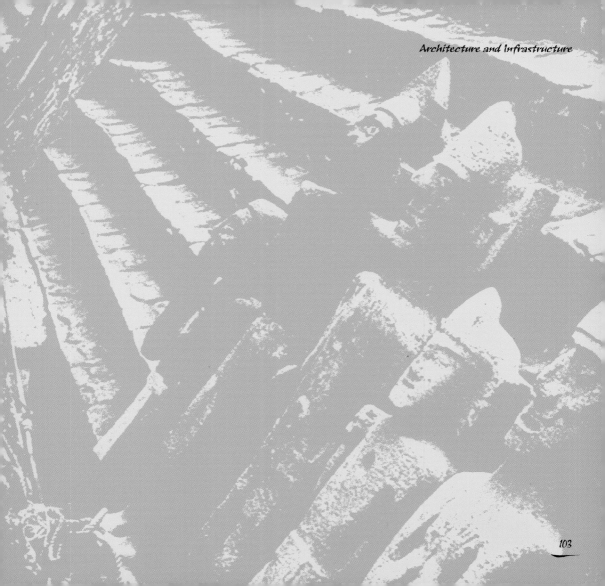

# Day-to-Day Life: Ballgames and Sacrifice

# *Olmec Society*

Olmec society was strictly hierarchical, ordered according to status and wealth. The kings, priests and skilled craftspeople, including sculptors, stone carvers, specialist builders and engineers lived in the urban centres while the farmers in the surrounding countryside produced food for them. Manioc, maize, beans and squash were the main crops; when necessary, their production was aided by an irrigation system. Cotton, tobacco and cacao were also grown. Fish and turtles provided the main source of protein, sometimes eked out with turkey meat and dog. During the annual flooding of the rivers, fish were caught in ponds which were kept stocked after the waters subsided. The floods also enriched the soil with silt. For their diversion, the Olmecs may have introduced the famous ballgame which was eventually played throughout Mesoamerica and sometimes further afield.

# Tarascan Society

The Tarascans were sophisticated bronze-workers and used the metal to make tools for farming as well as axes and chisels. In battle, they used bows, arrows and lances and protected themselves from their enemies with shields and armour made from cotton. They prized honey, cotton, feathers, salt and gold, demanding it in tribute from the people they conquered along with sacrificial victims, slaves and animal skins. There seem to have been three main social classes into which a Tarascan could be born: the class of the cazonci (the king) and the lords, the class of the nobility and the class of the commoners. The king was a diplomat, a representative of the gods, a judge, a war chief and the ruler of the capital city Tzintzuntzan. The heads of the different trades and professions all lived at his court. These included drum-makers, doctors, anglers, silversmiths and cup decorators.

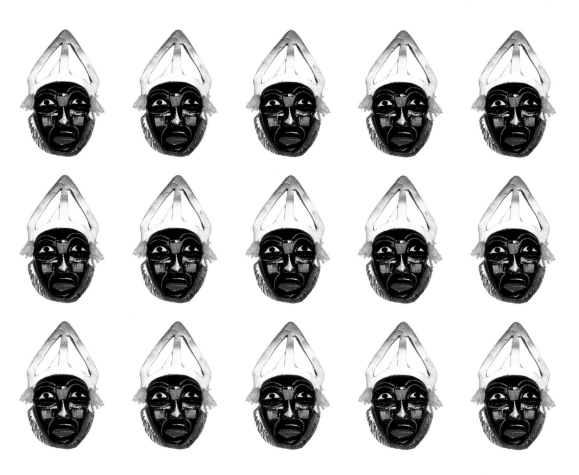

# The Ballgame

The Mesoamerican ballgame may have been invented by the Olmecs. Certainly, there was a ballcourt at the city of San Lorenzo and many Olmec figurines of ballgame players have been unearthed. All ages and classes probably played the ballgame which was used to resolve disputes, to mark important events including religious rituals and to predict the outcome of battles. Whoever lost the ballgame sometimes risked being sacrificed. The ball, which rebounded against the sloping or vertical sides of the court (known as the *tlachtli*), could not be touched with hands or feet and was typically hit with hips, knees or elbows. Players usually wore padded clothing and sometimes helmets. The aim was to score a goal by hitting the ball, sometimes regarded as a symbol of the sun, through a hole in a disc, as in basketball, or sometimes simply by hitting the disc. The game became hugely popular throughout Mesoamerica and a form of it is still played today in some areas.

# The Mayan Ballgame Story

At the end of the third creation there was no one left in the entire universe but Xpiyacoc and Xmucane, or the Grandmother and Grandfather as they are sometimes known. During the night, the old man and old woman produced twin brothers, Hun-Hunahpu and Vucub-Hunahpu. The brothers grew up but all they ever did was play dice and ball, dressed always in their finest ballplaying outfits. During one of their games, the lords of Xibalba (the underworld) grew angered by the noise they were making and irritated with the magnificence of their outfits. They summoned Hun-Hunahpu and Vucub-Hunahpu to a ballgame in the underworld, telling them to bring their ballgame outfits with them. The brothers set off for Xibalba, crossing raging rivers and forcing their way through calabash trees until at last they arrived at the main hall.

### The Underworld

The dark lords of the underworld set the brothers a series of tests before inviting them to a house where they could relax and smoke. The brothers were warned not to use up the tobacco or the pine sticks used to light it, but the next morning Hun-Hunahpu and Vucub-Hunahpu had nothing left to show their captors. Their punishment was death. Hun-Hunahpu was decapitated and his head set high in a calabash tree. For the first time ever, the tree grew fruit.

## Xquie

One day, a girl called Xquie approached the calabash tree to pick its fruit whereupon Hun-Hunahpu's skull spat on her hand, making her pregnant. When Xquie's father discovered her condition, he sentenced her to death. Xquie fled to Xbaquiyalo, Hun-Hunahpu's wife, who looked after her until she gave birth to Huanpu and Xbalanque. The boys turned out to have magical powers. They, like their father, loved the ballgame.

### Outwitting the Dark Lords

As luck would have it, the twins found Hun-Hunahpu and Vucub-Hunahpu's ballgame outfits. Putting them on, they began to play. Immediately, the enraged lords of Xibalba summoned the twins to their kingdom. However, when the twins entered the halls of the underworld they ordered a mosquito to sting each of the lords in turn. The moment each lord was stung, he cried out, whereupon the other lords called out his name, asking what was wrong. In this manner, the twins learnt the names of all the lords of the underworld, thereby gaining power over them. The lords of the underworld then tested the twins with tricks, but these twins were too clever for them. Eventually, the lords challenged Huanpu and Xbalanque to a ballgame. The twins won, making the lords so angry that they insisted on more challenges until finally, driven to distraction, they decapitated Huanpu.

### The Sun and the Moon

The lords of the underworld hung Huanpu's head high on a wall of the ballcourt. Undeterred, Xbalanque persuaded a toad to jump onto his brother's dead body and transform itself into his head. No sooner was this accomplished than the twins began to play ball once again with the lords of the underworld. The moment the game began a white rabbit ran onto the ballcourt, just as Xbalanque had arranged. The lords were distracted and, hurriedly, Xbalanque unhooked Huanpu's head from the wall of the ballcourt and gave it back to him. The twins now learnt that their deaths were inevitable. Nonetheless, they continued to outwit the lords of the underworld and in so doing managed to reduce their powers even more. At last, Huanpu and Xbalanque ascended to heaven where one was given the sun and the other the moon.

*The story of the hero twins is preserved in the* **Popol Vuh,** *the sacred book of the Quiche Maya.*

# Mayan Hierarchies

Mayan society was divided into several classes: the rulers, the priests, the commoners and the slaves. At the top of the hierarchy was the *halach uinic* or 'True Man', who inherited his title. If the *halach uinic* did not have a son, his brother would rule and if he had no brother, the council would elect another family member to the position. The *halach uinic* governed a particular district with the help of a council which included a local administrator called a *batab*. The towns which fell under the *halach uinic*'s control paid him tribute in the form of grain, honey, game, cotton, precious stones and sometimes slaves. The *batab* was not paid tribute but the commoners had to support him. The *batab* had two or three advisers called *ah-cuch-cab* who could overrule his decisions in the village council. There was also a chief of war known as the *nacom*.

# Mayan Beauty

The Maya admired long, backwards-sloping foreheads and long, flat heads. To achieve their ideal they would strap babies' heads between two boards a few days after they were born. The Maya also admired crossed eyes and so mothers would dangle objects immediately in front of their babies' eyes in the hope it would make them look permanently inwards. Dental inlays including round discs of pyrites or jade were also admired and sometimes women would file their teeth into points to appear attractive. Body decoration including tattooing and scarification was common, as was body paint which sometimes took the form of glyphic inscriptions. Poor women wore necklaces, bracelets, nose ornaments and lip plugs made from shell, amber or wood whereas women from the elite class wore similar jewellery made from jade. Men also wore ornaments including necklaces, earspools, nose and mouth pieces and headdresses. Many ornaments, especially earspools, were shaped like flowers.

# Mayan Food and Farming

The Maya farmed large clearings in the rainforest; where water was scarce, they built underground reservoirs for holding rainwater. Maize, their staple food, was grown alongside chilli peppers, beans and squash. Other crops included maguey, bananas and cotton. Agriculture was based on slash-and-burn farming which required that a field be left fallow for up to 15 years, sometimes after only two years of cultivation. Terraced hillsides might also be farmed. The Maya hunted for wild turkey, duck and deer although meat tended to be eaten only at ceremonial feasts. They kept bees in hollowed-out logs for honey and wax.

# Chocolate

Usually reserved for special occasions, chocolate was drunk by the Maya at least as early as AD 500 and was probably drunk by the much earlier Olmec people too. The Mesoamericans consumed chocolate as a bitter-tasting drink made from ground cacao beans, sometimes mixed with corn and chilli, and sometimes honey or other ingredients added. An officer of the Spanish conquistador Hernán Cortés noted that the Aztec ruler Moctezuma drank fifty flagons of chocolate a day. The word 'chocolate' may be derived from the Maya word *chokola'j* which means 'to drink chocolate together'. Cacao beans were used as a form of money and were traded over long distances.

# Aztec Social Class

Aztec society can be divided into four classes: the nobility, the merchants and luxury artisans, the commoners and the slaves. The nobility consisted of the supreme ruler called the *tlatonni* ('he who speaks'), who was elected from within the nobility and ruled until his death, the chiefs (*tetecutin*), who held high military and governmental positions, and the nobles (*pipiltin*), who occupied important political, religious or military positions and might also work as scribes or teachers. Although *pipiltin* inherited their status, it could also be achieved through bravery in battle or through training for the priesthood.

## Merchants, Commoners and Slaves

Next in importance to the nobles were the merchants known as *pochteca*, who were organized into guilds and traded over long distances – and sometimes acted as spies for the government. Also important were the skilled craftsmen, the *toltecca*, who worked with luxury materials such as feathers, sometimes in guilds, sometimes for the state. There were two types of commoner, the free commoners (*macehualtin*) who included farmers, fishermen and everyday craftsmen and the peasants (*mayeque*), who worked the land of nobles in exchange for part of the harvest. The *macehualtin* could keep the produce they grew, although the land itself was owned by the neighbourhood or *calpulli*. Even if commoners had any wealth, they were not allowed to show it. People became slaves (*tlacotin*) either through breaking the law or sometimes through gambling or poverty. Slaves could buy back their freedom and any who managed to escape and reach the royal palace without being caught were given their freedom instantly.

## Elite Aztec Warriors

In Aztec society, the most prestigious warrior orders were those of the eagle warrior and jaguar warrior. The eagle represented the sun and the jaguar the moon. They were usually full-time officers in the army, their ranks made up of nobles who had distinguished themselves in battle through taking numerous prisoners. Usually four or five captives had to be taken in one battle for someone to qualify. The warriors wore helmets in the shape of their respective animals; the jaguar warriors dressed in ocelot skins while the eagle warriors wore suits covered in feathers.

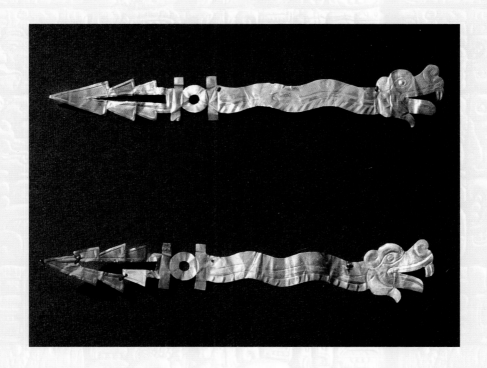

# Chinampas

The *chinampa* system was one of the Aztecs' most important methods of cultivation. They made extensive use of it in Lake Texcoco as well as Lake Xochimilco and Lake Chalco, and *chinampas* were considered so valuable that the Aztecs went to war to gain control over them. *Chinampa* agriculture consisted of making artificial islands by piling up mud from shallow lake beds and then planting them. Crops included maize, beans and chillis. Because part of Lake Texcoco was salty, fresh water was supplied to the *chinampas* by springs and eventually by aqueducts. The Aztecs believed that if the water flowed too high in an aqueduct, it could only be lowered if an important official were sacrificed and had his heart thrown in.

# Mesoamerican Clothing

The Mayans and Aztecs wore garments made from flax, feathers, wool and cotton, the commonest material in Mesoamerica. Clothing was very much an indicator of social status: the richer people might have rabbit skins incorporated into their dress while the poorer people would often have clothes made from maguey fibres. Dyes were made from shellfish, vegetables, indigo, wood, roots and fruits. Noble women were trained how to make textiles in special schools associated with temples, whereas poorer women would weave their family's clothes in their own homes. Dress usually consisted of a loincloth, cloak and sandals for men, and a skirt with a belt and a long sleeveless tunic for women. Noblemen's cloaks would be elaborately embroidered and emperors wore turquoise cloaks. Aztec priests usually wore black or dark green cloaks embroidered with designs of skulls and human bones. Soldiers and nobles would lace their sandals almost to the knee.

# Aztec Education

Aztec children were sent to single-sex schools from the age of seven, 10 or 14. There were two types of school, the *telpochcalli* or 'youth house' and the *calmecac*. Each neighbourhood had its own *telpochcalli* where the commoners were educated. The school was attached to the local temple and children were given religious training there as well as lessons in history, ritual dancing, singing and rhetoric. Public speaking was considered one of the most important skills for both men and women to acquire. Boys entering the *telpochcalli* would be given military training whereas girls would learn about particular religious rituals.

## The Calmecac

The *calmecac* was where the most promising boys and girls from the nobility were sent to be trained for religious, military or political leadership. Very occasionally an exceptionally intelligent commoner child might be chosen to attend. Each city had one *calmecac* for boys and another for girls. Students would spend all their time at the school, eating and sleeping there as well as studying. The curriculum included basic calendrical calculation, the use of the *tonalamatl* (a divinatory almanac), the significance and timing of festivals as well as history, maths, architecture, astronomy, agriculture, warfare and law.

# Sacrifice

Human sacrifice was common throughout much of Mesoamerica. It may have begun as a ritual associated with the harvest sometime around 7000 BC and from there it seems to have developed into a practice regarded as vital to the continuation of existence. The early Olmecs are believed to have sacrificed children, slaves and captives.

# Self-sacrifice

Self-sacrifice, including bloodletting, was widely practised in Mesoamerica, particularly by the Maya. The priests would feed the gods with their own blood, drawing it from their tongues, ears, lips or genitals through piercings. The more important the individual, the more blood was expected. In times of trouble, Mayan leaders would be expected to pierce their tongue or penis and pass a piece of rope through the hole. The Aztecs, including ordinary men and women, would pierce themselves with maguey thorns, then put the blood-covered thorns in a ball of straw called a *zacatapayoli* and place it in a ceremonial box in the temple. Sometimes they used needles or bone perforators to pierce themselves, usually in fleshy parts of the body like the earlobes, tongue or lips. Self-piercings were seen as a way of communicating with the gods on a very intimate level and as an indication of the individual's humility.

## Aztec Sacrifice

Mesoamerican sacrifice came to its peak with the Aztecs, who practised it on a vast scale. The Aztecs believed that the sun god needed human blood in order to survive. According to Aztec teaching, four suns (or worlds) had already been destroyed and only human sacrifice would prevent the destruction of the fifth. Human sacrifice became particularly important under the counsellor Tlacaelel (1397–1487), for both religious and political reasons. According to Aztec records, the practice was insitutionalized in 1484. At the dedication of Tenochtitlan's great temple in 1487, at least 20,000 captives were said to have been sacrificed in four days by eight teams of priests.

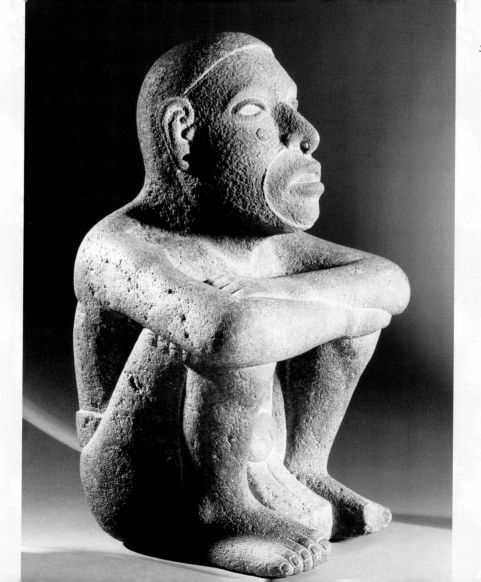

## The Ritual

Rather than killing their enemy on the battlefield, Aztec warriors conducted 'Flower Wars', bringing captives back for their priests who ritually sacrificed them. Sacrificial victims would also be paid as tribute by conquered peoples. The Aztecs believed that the braver the individual sacrificed, the more nourishing the gods found the sacrifice. The victims would be painted with blue chalk and taken to the top of the pyramid, or sometimes to the square facing the pyramid. There, they would be held down while their chests were cut open and their still-beating hearts pulled out and held up to the sun god Huitzilopochtli.

### The Victim

After a sacrifice, the victim's blood might be smeared on images of the gods or collected on strips of bark and burnt so that the smoke would rise up to the heavens. The victim's head would be cut off and set on a skull rack and his body might be thrown down to the bottom of the pyramid. Sometimes, the warrior who had killed the victim in battle was allowed to give out pieces of the victim's flesh and would receive tribute in return. It is possible, but by no means certain, that the flesh was sometimes eaten.

## Varieties of Sacrifice

Different gods warranted different forms of sacrifice. In rituals honouring the fertility god Xipe Totec, the victim would be tied to a post and shot full of arrows. The flowing blood symbolized the spring rains. The fire god Huehueteotl required that a newly wed couple be thrown onto the god's altar to burn. At the last moment they would be dragged from the flames and their hearts would be removed. The rain god Tlaloc was propitiated with the sacrifice of young children whose tears were needed by the god to wet the earth. At harvest time each year a female victim was flayed and her skin was worn by a priest who thereby took on the character of Teteoinnan, the earth mother goddess.

### The God of Night

Each year, a young man would offer himself in sacrifice to Tezcatlipoca, god of the night. For an entire twelve months, the youth would live a life of luxury. He would have four beautiful women as his constant companions and he would pass his time wandering the streets while playing a flute. At the end of the year, the youth would climb the pyramid, break his flute and die. Not all gods required human sacrifice, however. Quetzalcoatl, the feathered serpent, required the sacrifice of butterflies and hummingbirds.

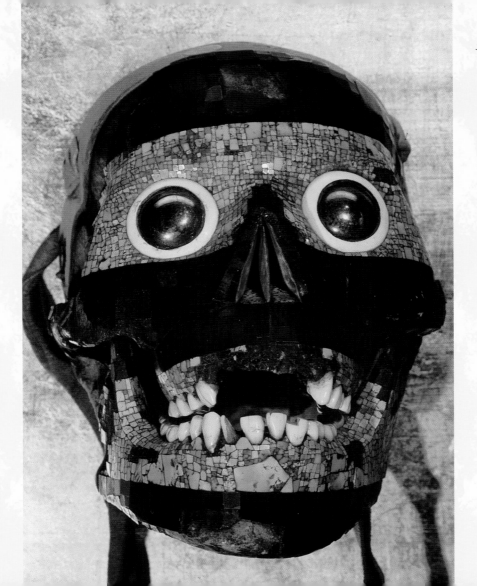

# Jade to Jaguars: the Arts

# Giant Heads

The Olmec culture is perhaps best known for having produced a number of colossal stone heads. They stand over 2 m (6 ft 6 in) high and were carved without the help of metal tools. Believed to be likenesses of ancient Olmec rulers, the heads are the oldest known monuments in Mexico. Many of them were defaced in some way, perhaps in some form of religious ritual after the leader had died. Some of the heads, made from basalt, weigh as much as 40 tonnes. One of the extraordinary facts about these vast heads is that they are found in areas where there is no stone from which they could have been carved. The ancient Olmecs must have quarried thousands of tonnes of stone in the mountains more than 80 km (50 miles) away and then moved it to the sites where they were displayed. Perhaps the stone was moved overland by sled, or maybe it was shipped along rivers on massive rafts.

# Massive Offerings

At their ceremonial centres, the Olmecs made
so-called Massive Offerings. They consisted of pits
lined with serpentine blocks. At the bottom of the pits
were mosaic pavements created to honour gods
or important leaders. When the mosaics were
finished, the pits were filled in — it is thought that the
Massive Offerings were hidden in order to give them
added symbolic significance.

# Were-Jaguars

One of the strangest and most mysterious creatures to have emerged from Mesoamerica is the 'were-jaguar', which seems to combine the animal and human. Figures and carvings of the were-jaguar were made by the Olmec people and were key to indicating to researchers that this was a previously-unknown civilization. They have round faces, down-turned, seemingly snarling mouths and sometimes thick lips and heavy-lidded eyes. Usually, they were found in the form of figurines of were-jaguar babies, or they might be carved into jade. The were-jaguar is generally thought to be a manifestation of the Mesoamerican preoccupation with jaguars, and perhaps associated with a myth to do with a male jaguar mating with a human. However, other suggestions have been put forward. Perhaps the were-jaguar is in fact a human child with a genetic abnormality and therefore, because of its abnormality, regarded as divine.

# Huastec Ceramics

Many Huastec pots were in the shape of animals or humans; bold red or black abstract designs were a favourite style of decoration. Sometimes clay figures had hollow legs filled with stones to produce a rattling sound when shaken or a whistle might be shaped like a bird.

# Huastec Sculpture

The Huastecs were skilled sculptors. They created intricate carvings on seashells which were often used as ear ornaments.

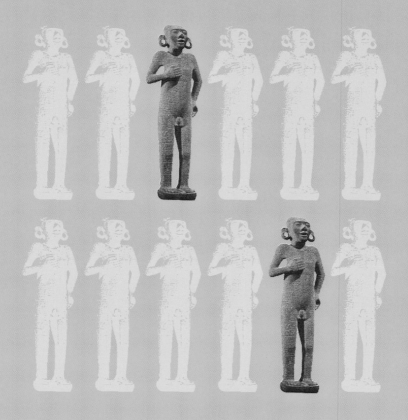

# Zapotec Art

The Zapotecs had many skilled craftsmen who created extraordinarily detailed urn carvings as well as engraved bones, gemstone work and elaborately painted and decorated tombs, particularly at Monte Alban and Mitla. Tomb murals were often of coloured figures, outlined in black, on a reddish background. A tomb at Monte Alban shows royal men and women walking in pairs towards the door of the tomb as if they are about to leave. Some of the figures have speech scrolls emerging from their mouths as if they are chanting. The Zapotec people are also renowned for producing carvings and sculptures showing humans in the guise of spirit animals.

# Totonac Art

Totonac art (now known as Classic Veracruz) is often associated with the ritual ballgame *tlachtli*, an immensely important feature of Classic Veracruz culture. The reliefs decorating the walls of the ballcourts exemplify some of the civilization's most impressive art while some of its most important artefacts are stone *hachas* (axes), *yugas* (yokes) and *palmas* (palms), all of which were associated with the ballgame. Some of the ballcourt reliefs show the ritual sacrifice of players. Clay figurines of ballgame players were also common. From the Remojadas region in Veracruz came hollow clay 'smiling face' figurines. These figures, decorated with black paint, include men, women and children; sometimes they are sitting, sometimes standing; all of them have smiling faces and some have filed teeth. The most well known Remojadas figures are those of laughing boys and girls with their arms raised high. The figurines may represent the use of hallucinogenic drugs in religious rituals.

# Masks

Masks were common throughout Mesoamerica but the artists of Teotihuacan made more than any other culture. The small Teotihuacan masks are usually realistic representations of people while the larger ones usually portray gods. Made of basalt or white and green onyx, the masks were sometimes covered with mosaics of coral or turquoise and might have eyes of mother of pearl or obsidian and teeth made from shells. The mouth area was sometimes coloured with a red pigment while the lips would often be parted. It is unlikely that the Teotihuacan stone masks were ever worn as they rarely had eye openings. They were probably hung from the walls of shrines.

## Trapezoid Masks

The famous Teotihuacan masks were
usually in the shape of a trapezoid
with broad faces and almond
shaped eyes.

# Murals

The Teotihuacans were famous for their murals. They covered all manner of subject matter from formal processions of deities and priests to jaguars, serpents, waterlilies, doves, scenes of dances and games and geometric designs. They were found in temples as well as in people's homes and could sometimes employ a highly sophisticated symbolism. The murals were made in the style of frescoes with colours added to a wet plaster base. The main colour used was red while other colours included white, orange, pink, blue, green and yellow.

# Mixtec Skill

The Mixtecs were famous for their metalwork. They cast beautiful gold, silver and copper ornaments and jewellery that were in constant demand. They also worked with precious stones, decorating objects such as masks and knives with mosaics of turquoise, coral and shell as well as elaborately carving wood, bone and stone weapons and ceremonial items. In the state of Puebla, a style of pottery known as Mixteca-Puebla emerged and spread throughout Mesoamerica, becoming an important influence on Aztec art. The pottery was decorated with brilliant orange, red and black designs of human and mythological beings as well as abstract patterns and finished with a glossy polish.

# Jade

Almost all Mesoamerican jade came from Guatemala and was composed of the extremely rare mineral jadeite. Mesoamerican jade ranges from pale green through blue-green to a virtually black colour. The Olmecs preferred a translucent blue-green whereas the Maya preferred a bright emerald green. As a colour, green was associated with rain, water and young growing plants. Jadeite was first used in Mesoamerica around 1500 BC for simple items such as beads; by 1000 BC the Olmecs were also using it for tools and figurines. When the Spanish conquistador Hernán Cortés arrived in Tenochtitlan, the Aztec leader Moctezuma gave him four jade beads, saying that each was worth two loads of gold. The Spanish were not convinced. The source of Mesoamerican jade remained a mystery until the mid-twentieth century; possibly the Mesoamericans concealed the mines, thinking that the Europeans would eventually recognize its value, or perhaps the mines were simply lost in the confusion of colonization.

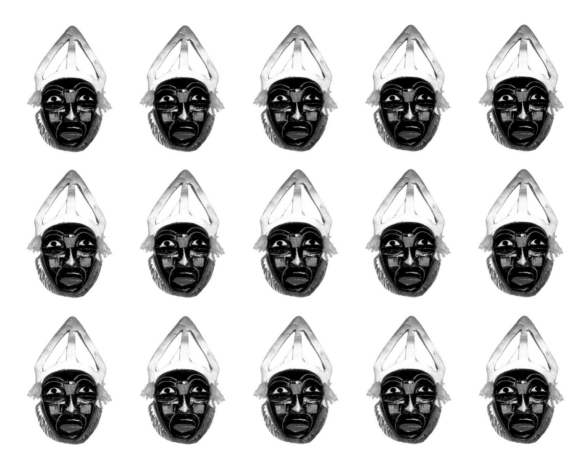

# Tarascan Art

Tarascan craftsmen may have been the earliest metalworkers in Mesoamerica, casting and hammering ornaments from gold, silver, copper and bronze. They also made jewellery from thin obsidian and rock crystal and created impressive ceramics and featherwork. Unusually for Mesoamericans, they worked extensively with gold plating.

# Jaguar Symbols

The jaguar was an important symbol of strength, ferocity and power throughout Mesoamerica. Jaguar carvings dating back to Olmec times show men dressed in jaguar skins and jaguar tails; sometimes jaguar paws were sculpted on images of Olmec leaders. The discoveries suggest that people believed they might become like a jaguar if only they dressed like one.

## Jaguar Power

The Maya clearly believed the jaguar had sacred powers and
stood in awe of the creature. Several Mayan deities were believed
to look like jaguars while the Mayan word *balam* means both
jaguar and high priest. The first historic ruler of Tikal (*c.* AD 292),
was called Jaguar Paw I and a Mayan carving shows a king sitting
on a jaguar skin while being crowned. Among the Maya, only the
kings were allowed to wear jaguar pelts.

According to the Aztec creation story, a jaguar performs an act
of great bravery by diving into a blazing fire to ensure the
creation of the fifth sun. In the Aztec army, the jaguar became
a symbol of one of the highest ranks, the Jaguar Warrior. In
order to reach such an elevated status a soldier had to be of
noble birth and to have taken at least four prisoners.

# Stelae

The Maya were highly skilled sculptors. They carved large, free-standing stones known as *stelae* with elaborate images of sumptuously dressed gods and leaders or scenes from myths and rituals, then decorated them with detailed symbolic designs or inscriptions. The most impressive *stelae* are found at Copan in Honduras. *Stelae* were not exclusively produced by the Mayans however, with most Mesoamerican cultures producing these symbolic and commemorative stones.

# Mayan Art

The Maya used many materials for their art including shell, bone, wood fibres and feathers, but they scarcely worked at all with metal. They made terracotta figurines and fine decorative ceramic tableware while stucco work was used for paving and for making relief panels. The Maya were also skilled textile workers, though this is only known from the illustrations that have survived on clay, murals and stone sculpture. A common theme found on Mayan ceramics is the royal audience; sometimes the name of the leader and his visitors are given in glyphs. Mayan artists belonged to the elite class and would sometimes sign their work.

# Toltec Art

The militaristic Toltecs were skilled craftsmen as well as renowned warriors. Their art, however, was often terrifying, perhaps intentionally so, in order to inspire the fighting spirit. Walls known as *coatepantli* were covered with carvings of serpents, and *tzompantli* — low platforms on which the heads and skulls of sacrificial victims were displayed — were often built near pyramids. There were also the threatening figures of the Atlantes, statues of warriors carved from giant columns.

# The Calendar Stone

The Aztec Calendar Stone or Sun Stone was carved in the fifteenth century and was discovered in Mexico City in 1790. It weighs almost 25 tonnes, has a diameter of about 3.7 m (12 ft 3 in) and a thickness of about 1 m (3 ft 3 in). The stone is dedicated to the sun god Tonatiuh, the fifth Aztec sun god. By performing regular sacrifices to the sun god, it was hoped that the current world could be sustained. At the centre of the stone, Tonatiuh is shown holding a sacrificial knife. The four squares around the central deity show the previous four suns: the jaguar, the wind, the fiery rain and the water. Originally painted red, blue, yellow and white, the stone also depicts numerous other symbols including the days of the Aztec month.

# Feathers

The Aztecs' most precious material was feathers. Brightly-plumaged birds were often farmed and their feathers, or sometimes the birds themselves, would be sent to the Aztec capital Tenochtitlan as tax or tribute. Feathers from birds such as the blue cotinga, scarlet macaw, yellow oriole and rose spoonbill would be made into fans, shields and headdresses. The feathers of more than 250 birds were used to make Moctezuma II's headdress. While large, colourful feathers were a sign of wealth and power, even ordinary people would use smaller feathers, pasting them onto their arms and legs for special ceremonies.

# Music

The Aztecs used music mainly for religious purposes, to accompany ceremonies, rituals and festivals. Musicians were members of the elite and underwent extensive training. A department dedicated to music within a *telpochcalli* was called a *cuicacalli* (house of chant). There were also priests dedicated to composing, supervising and correcting the chants. Despite their elevated position in society, musicians could be executed for playing a wrong note. Instruments included drums, rattles, ocarinas, whistles, flutes and even instruments made from large human bones. The instruments would usually be elaborately carved, often with religious images. Drums called *huehuetls* were made by hollowing out a log and stretching animal skin over one end. The musician could adjust the pitch by tightening or loosening the skin. *Teponaztli* drums were also made from hollowed-out tree trunks but these had two reeds on top which produced different vibrating sounds when struck with rubber-covered sticks.

# Poetry

The Aztecs thought poetry was the highest art form.
It was written by wise men called *tlamatinime*
(knowers of things), who were both poets and
philosophers. Poetry competitions and recitations
were held at festivals. 'Flower and song' was the
Aztecs' metaphor not only for poetry but also for art
in the widest sense. It drew attention to the Aztec
belief that, though life might be brief, the true and
the eternal could be found in art: though 'flower and
song' may perish, its essence will continue.

## The Flower Tree

Live here on earth, blossom!

As you move and shake, flowers fall.

My flowers are eternal, my songs are for ever:

I raise them: I, a singer.

I scatter them, I spill them, the flowers become gold:

they are carried inside the golden place.


(From 'The Flower Songs of Hungry Coyote' in
*Ancient American Poets*, trans. John Curl, Bilingual Review Press, 2005)

## With Flowers You Paint

With flowers You paint, O Giver of Life!

With songs you give colour, with songs you give life on the earth.

Later you will destroy eagles and tigers: we live only in your painting here,

  on the earth.

With black ink you will blot out all that was friendship, brotherhood, nobility.

You give shading to those who will live on the earth...

We live only in your book of paintings, here on the earth.

(From '*Romances de los señores de Nueva España*' in *Fifteen Poets of the Aztec World*,
trans. Miguel Leon-Portilla, University of Oklahoma Press, 1992. )

# Aztec Sculpture

The Aztecs produced thousands of stone sculptures. Using limestone, basalt or imported stone, they made a vast range of objects including large public images of the gods and goddesses, architectural decorations and small representations of everyday life. Stone sculpture was sometimes used for *cuauhxicalli* (containers for the hearts and blood of sacrificial victims) and calendar stones. The Aztec sculptors could create intricate details on very rough surfaces. They used tools made from stone and wood as well as sand and pumice stone for polishing surfaces. Most of their works were originally painted in bright colours.

# The Chacmool

'Chacmool' is the name given to sculptures typically found at Toltec and Mayan sites, such as Tula and Chichen Itza. The chacmool figure is always seated with its lower back flat against the ground, its upper back raised and its head turned to the side, almost at a right angle, with its legs drawn up and elbows resting on the ground. It holds a receptacle on its stomach that is thought to be for offerings of incense, human hearts, or other sacrifices. Chacmools may have symbolized fallen warriors delivering offerings to the gods.

# On First Seeing the Art of the Aztecs

'All the days of my life I have seen nothing that
rejoiced my heart such as these things, for I have seen
among them beautiful works of art, and I marvelled
at the subtle intellects of men in foreign places.'

(German artist Albrecht Durer (1471–1528) on seeing Aztec
material sent by Hernán Cortés to the Spanish king in 1520.
Quoted in: Eduardo Matos Moctezuma, *Aztecs*, Royal Academy
of the Arts, London, 2002, pp 48–50.)

# The Tizoc Stone

Towards the end of the fifteenth century, during the reign of the Aztec emperor Tizoc, a vast stone monolith called the Stone of Tizoc was carved. It stands over 1 m (3 ft 3 in) high and is about 2 m (6ft 6 in) in diameter. Fifteen pairs of figures are carved around the side of the stone, each consisting of an Aztec warrior taking a captive by the hair. Tizoc himself appears wearing the hummingbird headdress of the god Huitzilopochtli. A large solar disc with eight rays is engraved on the top of the stone. As well as celebrating Tizoc's victories, the stone was probably used for sacrifices.

# The Land of the Feathered Serpent: Religion and Belief

# Olmec Religion

The Olmec people's religious beliefs seem to have been dominated by a type of shamanism. By transforming into a type of animal spirit, known as a *nagual*, the rulers were believed to connect the natural with the supernatural world. Many of these *naguals*, particularly in the form of jaguars, appear in early Olmec art. The Olmecs also seem to have worshipped a creature known as the Great Serpent who was thought to have divine powers and to bring prosperity and growth to the Olmec people. The Olmecs also believed that the human body symbolized the three cosmic realms. The head represented the celestial realm, the body the terrestrial realm and the lower legs and feet represented the underworld.

# Zapotec Religion

The Zapotecs had an elaborate religious system in which great emphasis was placed on ancestor worship and human sacrifice. Their supreme creator god was known as Coqui-Xee, Coqui-Cilla or Pije-Tao, who showed himself in lightning, thunder and clouds. As the giver and sustainer of life, he symbolized the creative force. Other important deities included Cocijo, the equivalent of the Aztec rain god Tlaloc and Pitao Cozobi, god of maize.

# Teotihuacan Religion

The number of religious buildings and artefacts found in Teotihuacan suggests that the Teotihuacans were a very spiritual people. Priests were regarded as the representatives of the deities and, as such, had absolute authority. They were in charge of watching the movements of the sun and moon, the calendar and the religious ceremonies, including human sacrifices. The rain god Tlaloc seems to have been the city's most important deity but the jaguar, serpent, snail and bird were all important symbols. The jaguar represented religion and religious ceremonies, the serpent represented rivers, the snail represented fertility and birds represented the clouds.

# Mixtec Religion

The Mixtecs' most important deity was the sun god. Other gods were associated with war, health, human sacrifice, fertility, rain, wind and air. Religion was used to justify conquest and the taking of captives. Rituals, both private and public, were seen as important in order to maintain the balance between the natural and supernatural worlds.

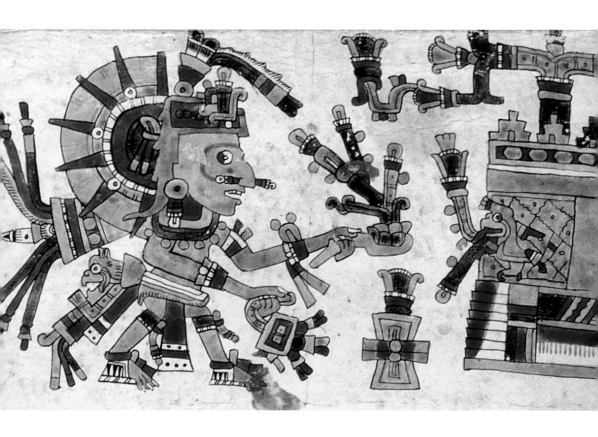

# Tarascan Religion

Tarascan religion centred on worship of the sun god Curicaueri or 'Great Bonfire', a deity similar to the Aztecs' Huitzilopochtli. The Tarascan king acted as Curicaueri's earthly representative; it was his duty to conquer new territory for the god and to supply him with sacrificial victims. If a decision was made to go to war, the priests at Tzintzuntzan, the Tarascan capital, would light huge bonfires which would be seen by the priests at the other eight Tarascan centres. They in turn would light bonfires until the whole region was alerted. Other Tarascan deities included the cloud goddess Cueravaperi and the agricultural goddess Xaratanga.

# The Mayan Creation Story

According to the *Popol Vuh*, in the very beginning there were two feathered serpents who lived together in the water and who, upon meditation, decided it was time to bring creation into being. So, as they lay next to each other, they planned the growth of the trees and the bushes and the creation of man. The first people were made from earth but they were intolerably stupid and they just crumbled away. The next people were made of wood but they had no souls and were ungrateful to the gods, so they were punished either by being drowned in a black resinous rain or by being devoured by demons. The next people, the ancestors of the Maya, were made from corn dough. At last, they had divine understanding so the gods decided to give them the urge to reproduce themselves.

# Mayan Gods

In early times, the Maya were probably nature worshippers. Although the belief that everything had its own life force persisted, the Mayan religion became increasingly complex with many gods and goddesses and numerous rituals including blood sacrifice, drinking, music and dance. In all, the Maya worshipped nearly 200 deities; some had both male and female identities and almost all of them had both a benevolent and a malevolent aspect. The most important Mayan god is Itzamna, the creator deity. His sons, the four Bacabs, are giants who hold up the sky at its cardinal points. Sometimes known as Chacs, the Bacabs control rainfall, thunder and lightning. They were an important source of information in divination ceremonies, in which ancestors as well as gods would be invoked. Another important deity was Kukulkan, known to the Toltecs and Aztecs as Quetzalcoatl.

## Itzamna

The moon god and founder of Mayan civilization,
Itzamna became the Mayan empire's principal deity.
A reptilian god, he was ruler of the night and the
father of the Bacabs. He brought his people maize
and cacao, invented books and writing and taught
them healing and the use of calendars. He is
represented as an old man with toothless jaws and
sunken cheeks.

## Ixtab

The goddess of suicide, Ixtab is sometimes shown
hanging from the sky with a halter looped around
her neck, her eyes closed in death and a black circle,
representing decomposition, on her neck. The Maya
believed that people who killed themselves went
directly to paradise.

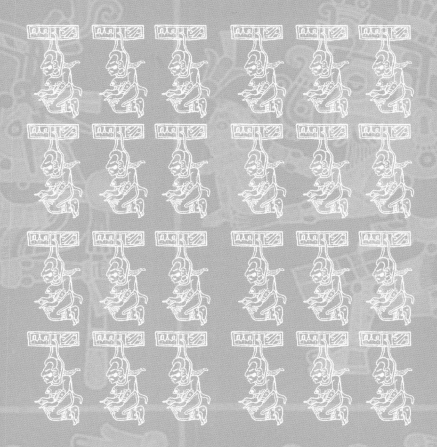

## Ixchel

The Mayan moon goddess was usually shown as an evil old woman crowned with a snake and wearing a skirt embroidered with crossed bones. She was associated with serpents and ill-luck and sometimes holds a large vessel from which she pours destruction down onto earth. In one tale, she runs off with the king of the vultures but her husband succeeds in finding his way to the palace, disguised, and takes her back. Ixchel was also the goddess of childbirth, divination, medicine and weaving.

## Ah kin

Ah Kin was the Mayan sun god who controlled drought and disease. He appeared as either a young or an old man. Each evening, Ah Kin descended to Xibalba, the underworld, or some say he turned into a jaguar god. His name means 'He of the Sun' or 'Day Lord'. He is sometimes cruel towards human beings.

## Ah Puch

The Mayan god of death, Ah Puch was also known as Hunhau and God A. He was shown either with the head of an owl or with a skull-type head and bony ribs. He presided over Mitnal, the lowest and ghastliest of the nine levels of Xibalba and fought Itzamna and Ah Mun in the battle between good and evil.

## Chac

Chac was the Mayan god of rain, thunder and agriculture. He was also known as Chaac and Chac Xib Chac. Sometimes he appeared in quadruple, as four separate Chacs, and these are sometimes regarded as manifestations of the moon god Itzamna. Like the Bacabs, each was assigned a corner of the earth. In the Yucatan, Chac was shown as an old man. In one ritual associated with the god, four young boys would be tied to the corner of an altar and forced to croak like frogs, creatures known to be harbingers of rain. The boys were probably sacrificed at the end of the ritual. Chac was the equivalent of the Aztecs' Tlaloc and the Zapotecs' Cocijo. He is usually shown with a reptilian face, two curling fangs and tears streaming from his eyes.

# Mayan Heaven and Hell

In Mayan cosmology, the *axis mundi*, the sacred *ceiba* tree, is the centre of the universe. The tree's roots reach down into nine-layered Xibalba, the watery underworld, its trunk stands in the middle world, inhabited by humans, and its branches spread out into the upper world which is supported by four huge gods, the Bacabs. The gods and the souls of the dead could travel up and down the sacred tree. At death, most Mayan souls fell into Xibalba. Heaven was reserved for priests and rulers as well as for people who had hanged themselves, been sacrificed or who had died in childbirth.

# Mayan Priests

The head of the Mayan religious hierarchy was called Ah Kin Mai, 'The Highest One of the Sun'. He ruled over the other priests, known as Ah Kin, 'The One of the Sun'. Priests developed the calendars, predicted events and organized festivals and rituals, including sacrifices. They were not celibate and boys often succeeded their fathers.

# The Myth of Ixchel and the Sun

One day, the Sun spied Ixchel, Lady Rainbow, as she sat weaving and instantly fell in love with her. When Ixchel's grandfather discovered the relationship he was furious. He threw himself at the Sun who immediately changed into a hummingbird and darted here and there, avoiding capture. Not realizing who the hummingbird was, Ixchel asked her grandfather to shoot the bird but when she saw the tiny body she realized what had happened. Distraught with grief, she nursed the Sun back to human form. The two lovers ran off, the goddess Ixchel by now transformed into the Moon.

## The Moon Disappears

As the Sun and Moon made their escape, the rain god threw a thunderbolt at them, killing Ixchel. With the help of dragonflies, the Sun gathered Ixchel's remains into thirteen hollow logs. Thirteen days later, twelve of the logs were opened and all the venomous snakes and insects now known on earth crawled out and populated the world. The thirteenth hollow log contained the Moon. Ixchel followed the Sun to his palace but the Sun soon became jealous, thinking she was having an affair with the Morning Star, his brother-in-law. The Sun threw Ixchel out of his home but then persuaded her to come back again. Time passed until once again the Sun became jealous and threw Ixchel out. Eventually, Ixchel became so annoyed that she abandoned the Sun and now she only appears when he is not around. Nowadays, Ixchel passes her time helping women through pregnancy and childbirth.

# The Five Aztec Suns

The Aztecs believed that four creations, or
'world-ages', had already come to an end
and that they were living in the fifth and final
creation. The current sun could be nourished
and sustained with the hearts and blood of
sacrificial victims, preferably those of
prisoners of war.

## The First Creation

The first creation was that of the Jaguar Sun,
*Nahui Ocelotl*, ruled over by the creator god
Tezcatlipoca, god of the night and sorcery.
During this creation, the world was
populated by giants who were eventually
eaten by jaguars, whereupon the world-age
came to an end.

## The Second Creation

The second creation was that of the Wind Sun, *Nahui Ehecatl*, ruled over by the feathered serpent Quetzalcoatl, god of civilization and learning. During this creation, the world was populated by humans who were transformed into monkeys. Powerful hurricanes brought this world-age to an end.

## The Third Creation

The third creation was that of the Rain Sun, *Nahui Quiahuitl*, ruled over by Tlaloc, the god of rain, moisture and fertility. During this creation, the world was populated by humans who were transformed into turkeys, butterflies and dogs. A great fiery rain brought this world-age to an end.

## The Fourth Creation

The fourth creation was that of the Water
Sun, *Nahui Atl*, ruled over by Chalchiuhtlicue,
goddess of running water. During this
creation, the world was populated by humans
who were transformed into fish. A great flood
brought this world-age to an end.

## The Fifth Creation

The fifth creation is that of the Earthquake Sun, *Nahui Olin*. This is the age in which we now live. It will end with great earthquakes. In one version of the story, the fifth sun arose when the humble god Nanahuatzin threw himself into a fire. However, the sun simply hung motionless in the sky until eventually all the gods sacrificed themselves in order to make it move.

# Tlaloc

The Mesoamerican god Tlaloc was probably worshipped as long ago as Olmec times but it was during the Aztec period, from the fourteenth to sixteenth centuries, that he became particularly important. Tlaloc brought both nourishing and destructive rain. He kept four huge jars from which he poured the rain, as well as disease, frost and drought, down to earth. Each year, young children were sacrificed to him. Their tears were seen as particularly auspicious. People who died by drowning, or were struck by lightning went to his home in the sky, one of 13 celestial planes.

# Chalchihuitlicue

The ancient Mesoamerican goddess Chalchihuitlicue was associated with lakes, rivers and seas. The goddess of youth and beauty, she was the consort of Tlaloc, the rain god and she released the flood which destroyed the fourth world. Chalchihuitlicue was portrayed as a river from which grew a prickly pear tree.

# Xipe Totec

'The Flayed God' was worshipped in many
Mesoamerican cultures though his cult was
particularly important to the Aztecs. He symbolized
the relentless circle of death and rebirth and he was
usually shown as a flayed young man wearing his own
skin. Each spring, people were sacrificed to him. The
victims were flayed alive and priests wore their skins
during rituals of renewal and rebirth. Xipe Totec
also had a military aspect as it was a rite of
passage for young Aztec warriors to
capture sacrificial victims for the
springtime festival.

# Xochipilli and Xochiquetzal

Called the Flower Prince by the Aztecs, Xochipilli was the god of maize, flowers, love and feasting. He was guardian of the souls of slain warriors. His twin sister, Xochiquetzal was similarly a goddess of flowers, fertility, games, dancing and agriculture.

# Huitzilopochtli

Huitizilopochtli, 'Hummingbird from the Left', was usually depicted as a man, painted blue and fully armed, with hummingbird feathers on his head. His name refers to the Aztec tradition that warriors slain in battle would return from the south (said by Aztecs to lie on the 'left' side of the world) reincarnated as hummingbirds or butterflies. Huitzilopochtli was the Aztecs' great sun deity and tribal god, associated with war and power, and patron deity of their capital city, Tenochtitlan. He is said to have inspired the Aztecs to begin their long wanderings from their homeland, Aztlan, which eventually brought them to the Valley of Mexico and Lake Texcoco. He shone so brightly that the Aztec warriors could only bear to look at him through the arrow holes in their shields. The bravest warriors were thus the ones who gained the best view of their god.

## The Story of Huitzilopochtli's Birth

As the small group of Mexica travelled southwards from their homeland, discord broke out between Coyolxauhqui, the moon goddess, and her mother Coatlicue, the earth goddess. To Coyolxauhqui's horror, Coatlicue was pregnant, the result of having gathered into her skirts a ball of feathers (traditionally believed to be the soul of a warrior) which had fallen from heaven. Coyolxauhqui told her 400 brothers, the stars of the southern sky, about their mother's condition, saying she had brought shame and dishonour upon the family. Together, the children hatched a plot to kill their mother.

## The Triumph of the Sun

When the travellers reached Snake Mountain, they paused for rest. Coatlicue, however, headed for the mountain's summit in order that she might perform her sacred rituals. Intent on carrying out their plan, her children followed close behind. As the children drew near, Huitzilopochtli spoke to Coatlicue from inside her womb, telling her not to worry. The moment the children attacked, Huitzilopochtli leapt from inside his mother, fully armed for battle. First, he sliced Coyolxauhqui into pieces and threw her body to the bottom of the mountain. Next, he tossed her head into the sky where it became the moon; that way Coatlicue might draw comfort from seeing her daughter in the sky every night. Finally, he attacked his brothers with his fabulous weapon the *xiuhcoatl* or turquoise snake. Terrified, the brothers ran away, leaving Huitizilopochtli in command. Each day, however, the battle between the sun and moon must be repeated.

## Huitzilopochtli's Shrine

As patron deity of Tenochtitlan, Huitzilopochtli's shrine stood on top of the Templo Mayor, along with that of the rain god Tlaloc. In order that the sun god might triumph in his daily struggle with the moon and stars, he needed to be nourished with the blood of sacrificial victims, preferably captives taken in war, and so sacrifices were performed in front of his shrine.

# Tezcatlipoca

Tezcatlipoca's cult was probably brought to central Mexico by the Toltecs towards the end of the tenth century. The Aztecs worshipped him as their god of night. He carried a magic smoking mirror that could kill enemies and enabled him to see into the hearts of men. He was often regarded as the supreme god of the Mesoamerican pantheon. The opposite of the spiritual Quetzalcoatl, he was a magician and shape shifter, the patron of royalty. Tezcatlipoca was usually depicted with a black band across his face and with a withered foot that ended in a mirror made of obsidian.

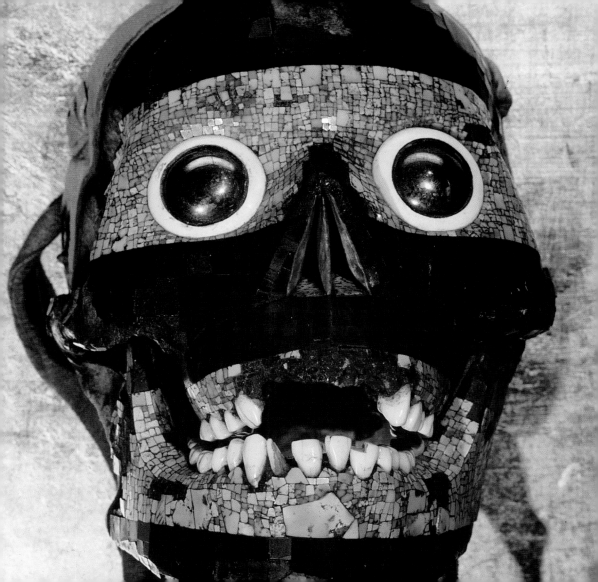

# Quetzalcoatl

Each Mesoamerican culture had its own gods, but
several gods were found throughout the region,
although sometimes known by other names. The
feathered serpent Quetzalcoatl, known as Kukulkan
by the Maya, was one such god.

## One Reed, Our Prince

The Toltec prince Ce Acatl Topiltzin ('One Reed, Our Prince') was the son of Mixcoatl, the Toltec ruler. Legend has it that Mixcoatl was murdered by the wicked Ihuitimal who then seized his throne. When Ce Acatl Topiltzin grew up he killed Ihuitimal and declared himself king. Ce Acatl Topiltzin was fair skinned with long dark hair and a beard. He had been educated at the shrine of Quetzalcoatl and claimed to be an incarnation of the god. Calling himself by the god's name, King Quetzalcoatl taught the people of Teotihuacan all their arts and sciences and instituted good and wise laws. He named all the mountains and all the seas, he discovered maize, he established the farming of maguey and he taught music and dance. He also helped with fertility problems and cured blindness, coughs and skin problems.

## Tezcatlipoca's Trick

In AD 968, King Quetzalcoatl moved the Toltec capital to Tula, bringing great prosperity and glory to their city. He banned human sacrifices and cleansed the city of all corruption and cruelty. However, the followers of the dark god Tezcatlipoca hated King Quetzalcoatl and set their demons on him. One day, Quetzalcoatl fell ill whereupon Tezcatlipoca transformed himself into a shrivelled old man and offered Quetzalcoatl a potion, promising it would cure him. Soon, Quetzalcoatl and all his attendants were drinking the potion which was, unknown to them, the alcoholic drink *pulque*. The king himself had outlawed drunkenness.

## Quetzalcoatl's Departure

When Quetzalcoatl discovered to his horror what had happened, he prepared to
leave Tula in shame. The year was AD 999. Before leaving he burned his palace,
turned the city's cacao plants into thorn bushes and buried his treasure in the
mountains. Then he set off with a small band of followers, some of whom froze to
death as they crossed the snowy mountain passes. Eventually, Quetzalcoatl
settled in Cholula. There he remained until, one day, he dressed himself in feather
clothes and a turquoise mask and set himself on fire. As he rose in flames to
become the planet Venus, he vowed that one day he would return.

## Kukulkan

According to Mayan tradition Quetzalcoatl sailed off across the Gulf of Mexico until eventually he landed on a beach on the Yucatán Peninsula. There, the Mayan people were expecting the return of their plumed serpent god Kukulkan and greeted Quetzalcoatl as his second coming. He became known as Topiltzin-Quetzalcoatl-Kukulkan and rebuilt the ancient capital of Chichen Itza. Eventually, Topiltzin-Quetzalcoatl-Kukulkan's enemies discovered his whereabouts and so he fled to Uxmal where he finally killed himself. According to one legend, he was buried under the Temple of the Dwarf.

## Quetzalcoatl and Moctezuma

When the Spanish conquistador Hernán Cortés arrived from overseas in 1519, the Aztec emperor Moctezuma is said to have been convinced that this was in fact the great plumed serpent returning to reclaim his throne. The Aztecs even dressed Cortés in the style of Quetzalcoatl, giving him a turquoise mosaic snake mask with a head fan of quetzal feathers.

## The Story of Quetzalcoatl and the Underworld

In one version of the creation story, Quetzalcoatl has an important role to play. In the beginning there was nothing but darkness, all but for Ometecuhtli, 'Lord of Duality' and Omecihuatl, 'Lady of Duality'. Together, they created all life and produced four sons, Quetzalcoatl, Tezcatlipoca, Huitzilopochtli and Tonatiuh. Quetzalcoatl was a kindly god but Tezcatlipoca was the god of evil and sorcery. Tezcatlipoca longed to light up the world and so he transformed himself into the first sun. Fearing his evil nature, the other gods persuaded Quetzalcoatl to strike him down. Quetzalcoatl struck Tezcatlipoca with a huge club and Tezcatlipoca plunged deep into the sea where he transformed himself into a jaguar. Under cover of the ensuing darkness, he devoured all the people and all the giants.

## Creating Humans

Quetzalcoatl now became the second sun; he made new people and ruled over the entire universe. One day, however, Tezcatlipoca stretched out his paw from the depths of the ocean and pulled his brother down to earth. This upheaval caused an immense hurricane which uprooted all the earth's vegetation and once again destroyed human beings, all but for a few people who were transformed into monkeys. The other gods then banished Quetzalcoatl and Tezcatlipoca from the sky and persuaded the rain god Tlaloc to be the third sun.

## The Sun and the Moon

By now, however, Quetzalcoatl had grown angry and he caused a rain of fire to descend and dry up all the rivers on earth. Once again, every human being was killed, all but for a few people who this time were transformed into birds. Quetzalcoatl then made the goddess Chalchiutlicue, 'Lady Precious Green' or 'Jade Skirt', the fourth sun. However, Tezcatlipoca was jealous and sent a flood to destroy both the sun and the earth. Once again, every human being died, all but for a few people who were transformed into fish. There was now nothing but darkness on earth once again. The gods assembled in the sacred city of Teotihuacan to offer up sacrifices in the hope that there might be light once more. Two gods, Tecuciztecatl and Nanantzin, prepared to sacrifice themselves. The poorer of the two, Nanantzin, dared to throw himself into the sacrificial fire first, and he became the sun. Then Tecuciztecatl cast himself into the flames, and he became a brilliant moon. To darken the light of the moon, the gods threw a rabbit at it creating holes on its surface which can still be seen today.

## Mictlan

Quetzalcoatl now descended to Mictlan, the underworld. There, he tricked Mictlantechutli, the god of the underworld, into letting him take back the bones of the people who had died. Back in the middle world, Quetzalcoatl created new humans by sprinkling the bones with his own blood. The Aztecs were therefore direct descendants of none other than Quetzalcoatl himself.

# Aztec Afterworlds

Upon death, Aztecs would enter one of four paradises in the underworld. The eastern paradise was for the souls of warriors killed in combat together with sacrificial victims — the souls stayed there for four years and then returned to earth as hummingbirds; the western paradise was for women who died in childbirth; while the southern paradise was for those who died of lightning or sickness. The paradise of the north was for everyone else. It took four years to reach this fourth paradise, called Mictlan. In order to help the dead along their way, they were buried in a squatting position with water and particular items, for example a jade bead, to help them overcome the trials they would have to endure.

# Carvings and Codices: Language

# Mesoamerican Languages

The languages of Mesoamerica are perhaps best known for their diversity. More than 20 language groupings are found in the region, with several different sound – and grammatical – systems. The best-known languages include those of the Mixtecs, Zapotecs, Aztecs, Totonacs and Kiche (or Quiche) Maya, while the Tarascan language is famous for being unrelated to any other in Mesoamerica. Quiche still has more than two million speakers and is the language in which the *Popol Vuh* was written; Nahuatl was the language of the Aztecs and Toltecs; and scarcely anything at all is known about the early Olmec language.

# Was Olmec the First Written Language in Mesoamerica?

No one knows for sure what language the Olmecs spoke, although it is generally believed to have belonged to the Mixe-Zoquean family, which is still spoken around the Isthmus of Tehuantepec. At the end of the twentieth century, Olmec artefacts dating back to 650 BC were unearthed. The symbols inscribed thereon are believed by some archaeologists to belong to an early writing system. If this were true, then the Olmecs could be said to have developed the first written language in the New World. However, other experts say that the symbols are no more than drawings.

# Zapotec Writing

Zapotec is one of the oldest writing systems in Mesoamerica, dating back to around 600 BC. More than 500 stone inscriptions have been found in the Valley of Oaxaca on monuments and the walls of tombs and the script spread much further afield. Zapotec writing records the fortunes of the Zapotec state between 500 BC and AD 700; many of the inscriptions deal with the deeds of ancient Zapotec rulers, as well as sacrifices, battles and so forth. On the Danzante slabs at Monte Alban the simplest inscriptions give merely a sacred calendar date, which is most likely the name of the person depicted on the slab. Zapotec script was used for 1,500 years but then slowly began to lose its hold, possibly as a consequence of the decline of the city of Monte Alban. By the tenth century AD it was being replaced by Mixteca-Puebla writing.

# Mixtec Codices

Seven Mixtec codices (painted, screenfold books) were saved from the Spanish conquistadors. The earliest of these dates back to the thirteenth century AD. The codices were written by Mixtec priests in pictographs and read from left to right. Most of them were made from deerskin coated with lime in order to give it a white appearance and then painted with inks made from plants and seeds.

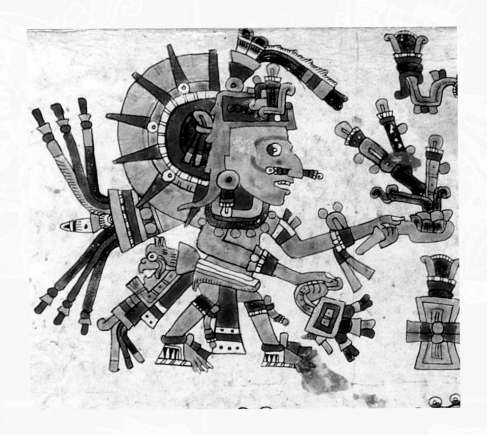

## The Nuttall and Vindobonensis Codices

The Mixtec codices recorded the divine descent of royal families as well as rituals, auguries and religious ideas. *Codex Vindobonensis* shows the activities of the original gods and ancestors including the Great Tree (Tree of Life) giving birth to the first Mixtec rulers. The deities of nature and creation associated with preparing the tree are also depicted. The *Nuttall Codex* shows many of the same people and places taking part in the great War of Heaven. It also contains nearly 200 representations of women, nearly all of them portrayed in responsible roles.

## Lord Eight Deer

The best-known story of the Mixtec codices is that of Lord Eight Deer, or Jaguar Claw, a warrior who rose to power in the eleventh century AD. Lord Eight Deer's epic history details his efforts to expand his realm as well as his numerous marriages. It is related in several codices, including the *Codex Bodley* and *Codex Zouche-Nuttall*.

# Mayan Glyphs

The earliest-known Mayan piece of text dates back to between 200 and 300 BC — the stone inscription has not, however, been deciphered. Mayan writing consists of hundreds of different glyphs (signs or pictures) and groups of glyphs. Sometimes they are in the form of humans, animals or other beings or objects; sometimes they are abstract designs, and as in Ancient Egyptian hieroglyphs, they can represent meanings or sounds. In a body of text, the most important glyphs are placed towards the centre of a group and are larger than the others. Less important glyphs are placed above, below or on either side of the main glyph.

## How to Read Mayan Texts

If there are two columns of glyphs, the text is usually read from left to right. When there are odd numbers of columns the first column is read down and the next two are read left to right or the first two are read left to right and the furthest right is read downwards.

# Mayan Codices

Four Mayan codices have been preserved. Three are in European libraries: in Dresden, Madrid and Paris. The last, the *Grolier Codex*, is in Mexico City, though not all experts believe that this fourth codex is indeed Mayan. Used by priests to interpret events and to conduct religious rituals, the Maya believed their codices were sacred books. They were also concerned with astrological, astronomical, agricultural and historical events.

## Book Burnings

The Mayan codices were written on long pieces of fig bark paper which were then folded like accordions and bound in jaguar skin. Most codices were usually placed in royal tombs. Apart from the four surviving codices, all other Mayan books either perished in the tropical climate or were burned soon after the Spanish conquest by Friar Diego de Landa, Bishop of Yucatán. According to the bishop, the codices 'contained nothing but superstitions and falsehoods of the devil'.

# Where and How?

Glyphs were carved on stone, on *stelae*, on the inside and outside of buildings, above doorways and on altars. They were also painted on ceramics, on ornaments made of stone or bone or on stucco walls. On codices, glyphs were painted in colour and protected with a white lime finish.

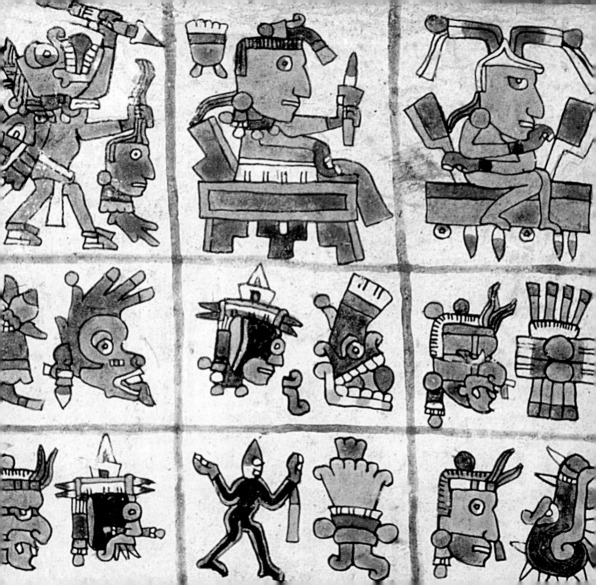

# The Popol Vuh

'This is the account of how all was in suspense, all calm, in silence; all motionless, still, and the expanse of the sky was empty.' These are the opening words of the *Popol Vuh*, the sacred book of the Quiche Maya, discovered at the beginning of the eighteenth century. Written in Quiche from 1554 to 1558 by a Mayan author or authors, it goes on to describe the creation of earthly beings, the actions of the gods, the origin and history of the Quiche Maya, the founding of the Quiche kingdom and the genealogies of the Quiche tribes.

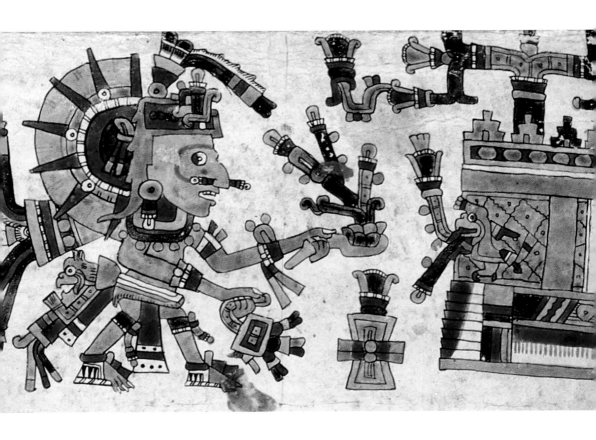

# Nezahualcoyotl

Nezahualcoyotl or Hungry Coyote (AD 1402–72) is probably the best-known poet and philosopher of ancient Mexico. In his writing, he struggled to come to terms with the mysteries of life and death but, more practically, he was a talented architect, a just law-giver and the enlightened ruler of the city of Texcoco which lay across the lake from the Aztec capital Tenochtitlan. Nezahualcoyotl began a prestigious library, designed magnificent botanical gardens and established an academy of scholars and poets. He was a founder member of the Triple Alliance with the Aztecs, while he himself came from the Acolhua people who rose to importance during the twelfth century AD.

# Aztec Writing

The Aztecs used pictographs (drawings and pictures aimed at communicating words or ideas), to record history, astronomical information and traditional tales. Each temple had a library of religious and astrological works. The administration of the capital Tenochtitlan required huge amounts of written work in order to keep track of taxes, tributes and trade; every year 24,000 reams of paper, made from the inner bark of fig trees, were sent to the city. Aztecs also wrote on stone, ceramics and textiles. Scribes or codex painters called *tlacuilos* drew the signs that gave the basic elements of the story and additional information would be added by the reader – the Nahuatl verb for 'to read' is better translated as 'to narrate'.

## Aztec Pictographs

The design of the figures shown in pictographs followed very particular rules. The head and feet were shown from the side, while the body was shown from the front. The scribe outlined the figures in black and then added the colours, mainly red, blue, green and yellow. Sometimes a varnish was used to add a final gloss. The Aztecs had not discovered perspective, so the most distant figures would be placed at the top of a page and the nearest at the bottom, while a figure's importance would be indicated by its size.

# Celestial and Earthly:
## Mesoamerican Science

# Olmec Calendars

By around 400 BC, the Olmec people seem to have been using two calendars. One, the ritual calendar, was based on a 260-day cycle. The number of days was possibly associated with fertility since it more or less tallies with the length of a woman's pregnancy. The other calendar was secular and lasted 365 days. Succeeding cultures developed the Olmec calendar.

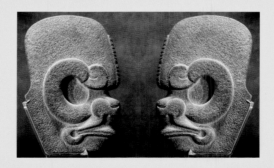

# The Cardinal Points

According to Mesoamerican cosmology the universe consists of five parts: the four cardinal points and a centre. These five points can be represented by the *quincunx* symbol, an example of which can be found at the ancient city of Teotihuacan, which was laid out in the shape of a vast *quincunx*. The Aztecs allocated everything, every creature and every object, to a particular cardinal point. Each cardinal direction had important symbolic value and was assigned a divine patron, colour, day and year. East was the region of fertility and life; its sacred colour was red. Symbols associated with the east included the crocodile, serpent and water. The north was a cold, dry region associated with death and the colour black. Symbols associated with the south included the rabbit, the lizard and the flower. The south was also related to the colour white, to the sun and to heat. Symbols associated with the west included the house, deer, eagle and the rain.

Celestial and Earthly

# Mayan Astronomy

Using only the most basic tools such as crossed sticks or shadow-casting
devices, Mayan astronomer-priests built up records which enabled them to
calculate precisely when the sun would rise and set, solar and lunar
eclipses and the movements of the planet Venus for centuries to come.
They also calculated that a year lasted 365.242 days. The *Dresden Codex*
contains an eclipse table that predicts when Venus will appear as the
morning star as well as other movements of the planets. Throughout
Mesoamerica, battles were often conducted according to the movements
of Venus and crops were sown to coincide with the appearance of
particular constellations.

# Archaeoastronomy

In Mayan cities, ceremonial buildings were often given an astronomical orientation. For example, at the spring and autumn equinoxes the sun might enter a small opening, lighting up the building's interior. At Chichen Itza on the Yucatán Peninsula, people still gather to watch the sun illuminate the steps of the great pyramid dedicated to Quetzalcoatl, the Feathered Serpent. Each year, at the vernal equinox (20 March) and autumnal equinox (21 September), the sun lights up the western balustrade of the main staircase in such a way that seven triangles appear, looking like the moving body of a serpent some 40 m (131 ft) long winding down the stairway to join the huge serpent head carved at its base. This image is meant to represent the great snake creeping down the sacred mountain to earth.

## Zenith Passages

Mayan astronomers attached
much importance to Zenith (or Zenithal)
Passages – when the sun passes directly over
the Mayan latitude – and would witness their
revered celestial body reaching its zenith
twice a year, casting no shadow from a stick
standing upright in the ground.

# The Mayan Calendar

The Maya had a calendar that was similar to most of those developed in
Mesoamerica. However, the Maya's was a more sophisticated example. It
consisted of a sacred calendar called the *Tzolkin*, which had a 260-day cycle,
and a secular or civil calendar called the *Haab*. Each day and each month
had its own particular deity.

## The Tzolkin

The 260-day *Tzolkin* consisted of a numbered 'week' of 13 days which interwove with a named 'week' of 20 days. (Thirteen was considered an auspicious, sacred number.) The names of the different days were believed to carry a deep meaning and the calendar was mainly used in divination.

## The Haab

The 365-day *Haab* consisted of 18 'months' of 20 days each, followed by five additional days, known as *Uayeb*. The *Uayeb* were known as 'days without names' or 'days without souls'. They were considered unlucky and were greeted with prayer and mourning. Fires were extinguished and anyone born on that day was believed to be doomed.

## The Long Count

In order that all dates might work from the same base date, the Maya used the

'Long Count', a continuous, linear count from a mythical date far in the past,

regarded as the beginning of the Mayan era, or even the beginning of the world.

The base date's equivalent in our own Gregorian calendar is either 11 or 13

August 3114 BC or 15 October 3374 BC. The earliest Long Count date yet found

was discovered on a fragment of *stela* in the Guatemalan highlands. It

corresponds to the Gregorian date 8 December, 36 BC.

# Mayan Names of Days

| Imix | | Waterlily |
| Ik' | | Wind |
| Ak'bal | | Night |
| K'an | | Corn |
| Chikchan | | Snake |
| Kimi | | Death Head |
| Manik' | | Hand |
| Lamat | | Venus |
| Muluk | | Water |

| | | |
|---|---|---|
| *Ok* | | Dog |
| *Chuwen* | | Frog |
| *Eb* | | Skull |
| *Ben* | | Corn stalk |
| *Ix* | | Jaguar |
| *Men* | | Eagle |
| *Kib* | | Shell |
| *Kaban* | | Earth |
| *Etz'nab* | | Flint |
| *Kawak* | | Storm cloud |
| *Ahaw* | | Lord |

# Mesoamerican Numbers

Counting in Mesoamerica was based on groups of 20 and known as vigesimal.
The system is thought to have developed from people counting their fingers and
toes. From as far back as 1200 BC, numbers were written down using bar and dot
notation; a dot represented 'one' and a bar represented 'five'. For larger numbers,
different people used different systems. The Aztecs, for example, used a feather to
represent 400. The Maya developed the concept of zero, considered to be one of
their most important achievements. A zero was represented by an oval shell.

# Aztec Cosmology

The Aztecs believed that the earth was a flat disc
surrounded by water, set in the centre of the
universe. There were 13 heavens above the earth
and nine levels of the underworld below. At the very
centre of the universe were Ometecuhtli and
Omecihuatl the Lord and Lady of Duality.

# The Aztec Calendar and the New Fire Ceremony

Like most Mesoamerican civilizations, the Aztecs had two calendars, one for the ritual year and one for the solar year. The ritual year lasted for 260 days and the solar year lasted for 365 days. Every 52 years these two calendars came into line with one another and the 12-day festival known as the *xiuhmolpilli*, the Binding Up of the Years or the New Fire Ceremony, would be held. Five days before the end of the 52nd year, all the Aztecs put out their fires, broke their old utensils and awaited the possible end of the world.

## The Last Day

On the evening of the last day of the cycle, a long line of priests would leave Tenochtitlan and climb Mount Huixachtlan, in the Valley of Mexico. Standing silently in the darkness, they would examine the stars and when the Pleiades constellation crossed the highest point in the sky they would know that the sun would rise to start another 52-year cycle. The fire priest would then make a fire on the chest of a sacrificial victim and carry the flame to a platform. The victim's heart would be thrown onto the fire and all the citizens would slice their earlobes with a knife and flick their blood towards the new fire on the hill. Runners would light fires from this new fire until, as legend has it, all the fires across the Aztec Empire were kindled from it. The next day celebrations would be held with sacrifices, feasting and a renewing of homes and belongings.

# Aztec Medicine

In 1552 Martin de la Cruz, an Aztec artist working in a Catholic mission in Mexico, finished working on the *Badianus Manuscript*, a book about traditional Aztec medicine. It was the first American document on herbal medicine and drew on knowledge passed down over thousands of years. The manuscript, translated into Latin by Juan Badiano, an Aztec from Xochimilco, consists of 63 folios divided into 13 chapters. It was written on paper and bound in red velvet. When it was finally completed, the *Badianus Manuscript* was sent to King Charles V at the Spanish Court, where it was placed in the Royal Library. It later found its way to the Royal Apothecary, then to the library of Cardinal Francesco Barberini, nephew of Pope Urban VII, and from there to the Vatican Apostolic Library where it was discovered by a historian in 1929.

## Herbal Cures

The *Badianus Manuscript* describes 204 medicinal 'herbs' from small plants to large trees. In all, 184 plants and trees are depicted in brightly-coloured illustrations. Each of the manuscript's 13 chapters aims to deal with a 'family' of illnesses, covering close to 100 afflictions in all, beginning with those of the scalp and head and working downward to the feet. Leprosy and 'tubercles of the breast' are dealt with along with more everyday complaints such as 'fetid breath' and 'rumbling of the abdomen'. Like European works on herbal medicine of the time, the *Badianus Manuscript* also demonstrates a belief in the medicinal power of animal body parts and precious stones.

## Apothecaries

In a letter to King Charles V of Spain, Hernán Cortés described the Aztec capital Tenochtitlan as having 'herb sellers where there are all manner of roots and medicinal plants that are found in the land. There are houses, as it were, of apothecaries where they sell medicines made from these herbs both for drinking and for use as ointments and salves.'

## Moctezuma's Garden

In the fifteenth century, the Aztec emperor Moctezuma I (*c.* AD 1397–1469) developed the Huaxtepec botanical garden. It had a circumference of about 10 km (6.2 miles) and held more than 2,000 medicinal trees, shrubs and herbs. Academic priests experimented with plant derivatives from the garden and looked after the nobility. A chapter in the *Badianus Manuscript* called 'Trees and Flowers for the Fatigue of Those Administering the Government and Holding Public Office' promises that 'indeed these medicaments bestow the bodily strength of a gladiator, drive weariness far away, and finally, drive out fear and fortify the human heart.'

## Spain's Reaction

The Spanish were astonished at the large number of herbs used by the Aztecs and at the size and variety of their botanical gardens. Many Aztec medical practices were more effective than those used by early Spanish doctors. Charles V of Spain sent physicians and other scientists to study Aztec medicine. According to the Spanish Catholic priest Motolinia, 'They have their own skilled doctors who know how to use many herbs and medicines which suffices for them. Some of them have so much experience that they were able to heal Spaniards, who had long suffered from chronic and serious diseases.'

## Treatments

Both Aztec men and women practised as doctors, treating illnesses with a wide variety of medicines and treatments. The medicines in the *Badianus Manuscript* came from animal, vegetable and mineral sources. Usually, they were made from barks, flowers and roots. One of the more powerful painkillers was *argemone grandiflora*, closely related to the opium poppy. Healing stones were also used: heat in the region of the heart was treated with beryl, 'emerald' (probably jade in reality) and turquoise; fevers were treated with emerald; gout was treated with pearl and emerald.

# Man and Cosmos

The Aztecs lived in a precarious universe in which it was vital for good and evil to be kept in balance. Human behaviour was believed capable of affecting the equilibrium of the universe and, conversely, the movement of the planets was believed capable of affecting the health of humans. The importance of balance extended to health in other ways, too: a balanced diet was considered of utmost importance for physical well-being.

# The Gods and Disease

One of the first treatments for illness was prayer and then, perhaps, sacrifice. However, if the gods were thought to have inflicted illness on an individual for committing a particular sin, then confession was deemed necessary before any hope of a cure might be held out. If, for example, somebody sought a cure for illness caused by sexual immorality then confession before the goddess Tlazolteotl would be necessary. The goddess would eat the sin, thereby cleansing the sinner. Confessions were also made before the god Tezcatlipoca. After confession, penances would be imposed.

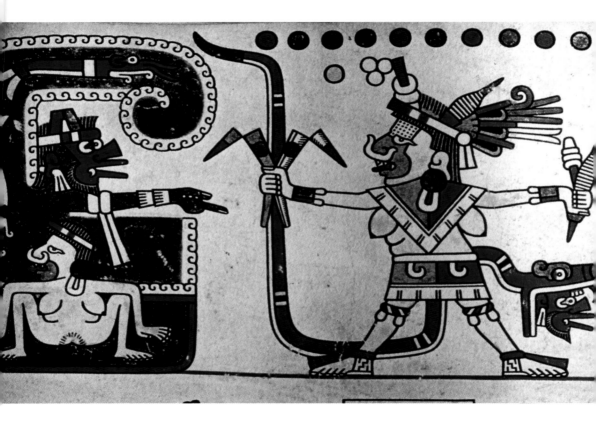

Celestial and Earthly